The 90s Vegetarian

The 90s Vegetarian

Ursula Ferrigno

MEREHURST

I am indebted

. . . to my grandmother, Genoveffa Ferrigno, for sharing her secrets

. . . to my mother for her interest shown and for helping me keep my feet firmly on the ground

. . . to my father for the love of excellent fruit and vegetables

. . . to my friends in Italy who have been so hospitable

. . . to Michele Barlow, my assistant, for all the fun we have had working together

I would like to thank *Gill MacLennan* my managing editor at Merehurst for making this book possible; for her permanent good spirits, energy, enthusiasm and encouragement that kept me fired. My book has been a joy to write thanks to Gill.

Also thanks to *Susanna Tee* for her dedication and excellent editing. For her great sense of fun and humour throughout; and also her conscientious attitude.

Published in 1994 by Merehurst Ltd
Ferry House, 51–57 Lacy Road, Putney, London SW15 1PR
Copyright © Ursula Ferrigno

ISBN 1 85391 309 X

Managing Editor: **Gill MacLennan**
Edited by **Susanna Tee**
Designed by **Lisa Tai**
Photography by **Ian O'Leary**
Styling by **Marian Price**
Illustrations by **Ken Cox**
Food for Photography by **Kathy Man**

Typesetting by Litho Link Ltd, Welshpool, Powys
Colour separation by Fotographics Ltd U.K.
Printed in Italy by G Canale & C SpA

I enjoy food and would love to think that I could pass on some of my enthusiasm to you. I hope therefore that my recipes excite you and that you want to rush out, buy the ingredients and start preparing them!

I have never thought of myself as a vegetarian, in fact I have often said I don't like vegetarian food as it can be brown and heavy. However, as an Italian who has grown up with a plentiful supply of fresh vegetables, herbs, fruits, nuts, interesting breads, grains, pulses and, of course, an enormous variety of pasta, only now do I realise that I am a meat free cook.

Whether you are new to vegetarian cookery or have been cooking vegetarian meals for years, I hope my recipes open up a whole new world of dishes to you. You do not even have to be vegetarian to appreciate them. I have certainly enjoyed collecting the recipes together for you and hope you enjoy cooking and eating them.

Ursula Ferrigno

Contents

Breakfasts 11

Figs in orange juice with toasted almonds

Hot cinnamon toast

Vitality spread

Rosemary and basil buttered toast with grilled
cherry tomatoes

Buckwheat pancakes

Zesty fruit and nut muffins

Apricot, fig and raisin balls rolled in sesame seeds

· Fruity porridge

Peachy yogurt shake

Warming hot chocolate

Banana and honey super shake

Hot apple juice with cinnamon, lemon and cloves

Espresso with amaretto and cream

Light Lunches 19

Warm marinated millet salad

Mange-tout, cannelloni and almond salad

Carrot, cheese and parsley sandwich with mayo

Beetroot and feta sandwich with parsley

Sun dried tomato pesto and pickled aubergine
open sandwiches

Roasted red pepper, cream cheese and rocket
sandwich

Fried mozzarella sandwiches

Broad beans and mint with gorgonzola dressing

Baked aubergine, olive and mozzarella sandwich
with basil

Cheesey carrot and nut bites with sesame seeds

Roasted tomatoes on toast with goats' cheese

Warm creamy courgette and spinach toasts

Bean sprout salad with nuts and raisins

Tomato and mint salad

Mushroom crostini with leeks and artichokes

Rocket and almond pesto on rye toasts

Roasted garlic and dolcelatte toasts

Bitter leaves with romesco dressing

Pickled red onion and avocado sandwich

Baked potatoes

Tomato, hazelnut and thyme filling

Poppy seed, celery, gorgonzola and chive filling

Celeriac and pecorino filling

Cabbage, mushroom and egg filling

Roasted red pepper and spinach filling

Midweek Meals 35

Fennel under a garlic cheese crumb

Vegetable stock

Artichoke, lemon and almond soup

Tangy tomato soup with lemon grass

Rice noodle cloud with stir-fried vegetables

Baked shallots with creamy broccoli

Deep fried risotto with shallots, orange rind and
mozzarella

Chicory rolls

Roasted cherry tomatoes with red onions, spinach
and cheese sauce

Giant stuffed mushrooms with pine nuts and sage

Bread gnocchi with rosemary and chervil

Risotto with asparagus, basil and peas

Baked baby peppers

Penne with pumpkin and pecorino

Potato croquettes

Ricotta and nutmeg dumplings with gorgonzola sauce

Risotto with raisins and pine nuts

Pasta with garlic, walnut and rocket sauce

Baked beets with a nut and cheese crumb

Pumpkin fritters with sage and parmesan

Hot broad beans and artichokes with chilli and herbs

Radicchio risotto

Rigatoni with garlic, rosemary and mushrooms

Broccoli and cauliflower with parmesan batter

Penne with pepper and pistachio sauce

Tagliatelle with saffron and mascarpone sauce

Baked aubergines with herby spinach and tomato
middles

Leek and tomato soup with crusty bread and basil

Pasta and bean soup

Aubergine rolls with goats' cheese and tomato

Mushroom burgers with leeks and blue cheese

Italian green lentil soup

Chestnut soup with chick peas

Sprouted beans with chinese leaf, ginger and
coconut

Weekend Eating 63

Roasted peppers with a pine nut and sultana stuffing
Parsley and mozzarella calzone
Tagliatelle in a fresh basil and walnut sauce
Chickpea stew with mediterranean vegetables
Hot asparagus with red pepper sauce
Spinach and cheese crespolini
Dolcellatta and lemon dressing
Parsnip, leek and coriander soup
Cold peppers stuffed with celery
Layered courgette and barley tortino
Fried four-cheese ravioli
White pizza with two cheeses and basil
Baked onions with a parsley and parmesan stuffing
Roasted red pepper tart
Radicchio and pecorino pizza

Having Friends Round 79

Deep fried caper-stuffed olives
Glogg
Mumma
Creamy corn tart with chilli and coriander
Char-grilled vegetables layered with cheeses
Leek, thyme and pistachio souffles
Hollandaise sauce
Fresh pasta with spinach, nutmeg and pine nuts
Polenta pie
Artichoke tart with gruyere
Celebration pizza
Potato and mushroom layer cake
Potato mountain pie with rosemary
Fat freddies pumpkin
Green sauce with capers and herbs
A cake of aubergine and courgettes
Shallot, spinach and mushroom tian
A cake of pasta and spinach
Grandmother Furiani's radicchio lasagne
Mushroom lasagne with roasted peppers
Apple, almond and soured cream cake
Wicked coffee fudge pudding
Honey ice cream
Boozy stuffed prunes drizzled with chocolate
Chocolate polenta cake
Baked chocolate cheesecake with vanilla and pecans

Chocolate and chestnut torte
Black grape cake with olive oil
Dried plum gnocchi with cloves
Hot spiced bananas with amaretto cream
Date and cognac ice cream
Fragrant almond cake
Dried pears, peaches and figs in red wine
Zesty souffles with apricot sauce
Baked peaches with amaretti
Pecan meringue cake with caramelised apples

Cooking for Pleasure 115

Rustic walnut bread
Sour dough bread
Focaccia
Grissini
Potato pizza bread
Flattened bread filled with spinach and olives
Prune and chocolate bread
Amaretti
Home-made toasted almond butter
Sweet milk bread with cumin and orange
Rum plum bread
Brandy, date and orange cream cheese
Mrs Ferrignos featherlight walnut scone
Taralli
Ciabatta
Florentines
Banana curd
Fresh egg pasta
Sun dried tomato puree
Coriander, mint and chilli chutney
Fragrant salt
Pickled red onions
Pickled pumpkin
Pickled aubergines
Fruity olive pate
Lemon grass oil
Sun-dried tomato pesto
Tarragon and pecan pesto
Rocket pesto

Recipe index

The Storecupboard

A well stocked store cupboard (and refrigerator and freezer too) not only save you endless shopping trips but also means you are able to make a meal at a moment's notice. These are the ingredients that I consider essential for a storecupboard.

Pasta I keep a large variety of dried pasta in various shapes and sizes (De cecco is my favourite brand). It is an integral part of our 90s lives, being economical, nutritious, quick to prepare, versatile and filling. When buying pasta, check on the packet that it is made from 100 per cent durum wheat or states *semola di grano*. When it contains egg it will also state *all'uovo*. Choice is very much personal taste but as a general rule, use thin pasta for fairly thick sauces, hollow or twisted shapes for chunky sauces, wide flat noodles for rich sauces and delicate shapes for light sauces. When buying pasta, check the date marking and store in airtight containers in a cool, dark place.

Grains Pot barley; '00' Italian flour for pasta making; strong flour for breadmaking; plain white flour for cakes, pastries and sauces; wheatmeal (85% extraction) flour for pastry, arborio (risotto) rice; basmati rice; porridge oats; semolina; polenta.

Pulses Canellini, pinto, red kidney and borlotti beans (both dried and canned); chick peas; red and green lentils.

Sugars Icing, caster, unrefined soft brown, demerara and muscovado sugar; vanilla sugar (made by leaving a vanilla pod in a jar of caster sugar).

Nuts and Seeds Hazelnuts; pine nuts; ground, flaked and blanched whole almonds; sunflower seeds. (Store in the refrigerator or freezer to preserve their vitamin E content).

Oils Walnut and hazelnut oil (stored in the refrigerator); extra virgin olive oil for dressings; olive oil for frying.

Cans Tomatoes; artichoke hearts; different sorts of beans; chick peas; lentils.

Bottles and Jars Balsamic vinegar; red, white and cider wine vinegar; green and black olives; capers; sun-dried

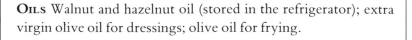

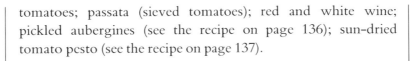

tomatoes; passata (sieved tomatoes); red and white wine; pickled aubergines (see the recipe on page 136); sun-dried tomato pesto (see the recipe on page 137).

HERBS Fresh herbs have a much better, truer flavour than dried herbs and most can be easily grown on a window sill – inside or out – or in the garden. Keep some dried or frozen herbs such as bay leaves, rosemary, oregano, sage and thyme for emergencies. Garlic, although not a herb but a member of the onion family, is used as a flavouring ingredient in the same way as fresh herbs. It will keep in a cool place for about six weeks.

SPICES Peppercorns; fennel seeds; whole nutmeg; gound cinnamon; cloves; saffron; sesame seeds, poppy seeds; peperon cino (small chilli peppers).

DAIRY PRODUCTS Although perishable and should therefore be stored in the refrigerator, these ingredients usually have a good shelf life. Free-range eggs; Greek yogurt; butter; mature Cheddar cheese, goats' cheese and one or two hard finely grained cheeses, known as *grana*.

These *grana* cheeses include **Parmesan**, the king of Italian cheese. Genuine *Parmesan* can only be made in Emilia and has the full title of *Parmigiano-Reggiano* which must be stamped on its rind. It is expensive as it takes at least 2 years to mature but a little goes a long way. **Grana Padano** is made in larger quantities than *Parmesan* but is not matured for as long and therefore does not have such a distinctive full flavour. **Pecorino** is a cheese made from Ewe's milk. There are many varieties but **Pecorino Romano** is considered the best. It is aged from between 6–8 months and is stronger, more tangy and saltier than Parmesan. Lastly, **Pecorino Sardo** is made in Sardinia and is not quite as strong as Romano. Store hard cheese wrapped in muslin to allow it to breath.

Cheeses are usually made with animal rennet and therefore not suitable for the strict vegetarian. However, the range of cheeses available made with vegetable rennet – including Parmesan – is increasing so look out for them if this is important to you.

MISCELLANEOUS Tubes of tomato puree; packets of dried porcini (wild mushrooms); coarse sea salt; plain chocolate; cocoa powder; dried fruits such as apricots, prunes and dates; coffee beans; tea; herbal tea; Marmite; Miso; tahini; jams; honey; natural vanilla essence.

Breakfasts

The first meal of the day is important, vital in fact, to sustain you through a long, busy day. This doesn't mean you have to produce a large meal or spend a lot of time on it. Anything – however small, is better than nothing.

This chapter is full of some of my favourite start-the-day recipes.

There are refreshing fruit dishes, warm muffins and pancakes, traditional favourites such as fruity porridge and hot cinnamon toasts and several vitality drinks. All make a nutritious breakfast and a good start to the day.

Make time for them.

FIGS IN ORANGE JUICE WITH TOASTED ALMONDS AND NATURAL YOGURT

Dried figs and almonds are a fantastic source of calcium. Orange juice is full of vitamin C. Mix together for a good start to the day!

SERVES 4
20 dried figs
2 fresh oranges
50 g (2 oz) flaked almonds
low fat natural yogurt, to serve

1 Nip the tops off the figs. Squeeze the juice from the oranges then soak figs overnight in the orange juice. Make sure the figs are covered in juice – if they are not, top up with a little water.

2 After 24 hours, the figs will be plump and juicy. Put in a saucepan and simmer for 15 minutes, until tender.

3 Toast the almonds on a sheet of foil under the grill, turning them frequently. To serve, sprinkle the almonds over the figs and top with yogurt.

• Thin skinned oranges have more juice than those with thick skins and if you warm them first, you will get the juice out of them more easily.

HOT CINNAMON TOAST

These toasts are crisp on the outside and soft and buttery in the middle. Serve warm.

SERVES 2 – 3
three 15 cm (¾ in) slices of white bread
  (preferably home-made)
40 g (1½ oz) unsalted butter
2 teaspoons ground cinnamon
40 g (1½ oz) demerara sugar

1 Preheat the oven to 190C (375F/Gas 5). Cut the crusts off the bread and cut each slice into 4 strips. Melt the butter. In a dish stir together the cinnamon and sugar.

2 Working with a strip of bread at time, turn the strips quickly in the butter, coating them on all sides and letting any excess drip off. Turn them quickly in the cinnamon sugar, coating on all sides.

3 Lightly butter a baking tray and bake the strips in the preheated oven for 10 minutes. Turn and bake for a further 10 minutes.

• For the freshest flavour, I like to grind cinnamon sticks in a coffee grinder. The flavour is much more pungent than ready-ground cinnamon.

VITALITY SPREAD

I always put a dish of this out for breakfast as an alternative to butter or margarine.

SERVES 4
3 tablespoons miso
3 tablespoons light tahini
bread, toast or rice cakes, to serve

1 Mix miso and tahini together until well blended. Spread thinly on bread, toast or rice cakes.

2 If necessary, cover the spread and store in the fridge, as if it were margarine then use when needed.

• Try to use light tahini as it is sweeter than the dark variety because the husks of the sesame seeds have been removed.

ROSEMARY AND BASIL BUTTERED TOAST WITH GRILLED CHERRY TOMATOES

It's the weekend, you've risen later than normal – this makes a great brunch.

SERVES 4

20 cherry tomatoes

50 g (2 oz) butter

sprig of rosemary

handful of fresh basil

4 slices of ciabatta or continental bread

salt and pepper

1 Preheat the oven to 200C (400F/Gas 6). Put the cherry tomatoes on a baking tray and bake for 12 minutes, until softened and the skins are split.

2 Meanwhile, prepare the butter. Put the butter in a bowl and soften with a wooden spoon. Chop the rosemary leaves and tear the basil. Add to the softened butter and mix well until well incorporated.

3 Toast the bread on both sides and while still hot, spread with the herb butter.

4 Place 5 baked cherry tomatoes on each slice of toast. Squash in lightly with a fork then season with salt and freshly ground pepper. Serve hot.

• **This really tasty breakfast is also delicious served with shavings of pecorino cheese. Use a potato peeler to shave the cheese into flakes. Flash under the grill until just melting.**

BUCKWHEAT PANCAKES

Buckwheat is a staple grain of Russia. It has a lively nutty flavour, excellent for the winter months. Look out for it in health food shops. These pancakes are quick to make. Serve with butter and your favourite jam.

SERVES 4

50 g (2 oz) buckwheat flour

50 g (2 oz) plain flour

2 teaspoons baking powder

1 teaspoon honey

1 egg

150 ml (¼ pint) milk

2-3 tablespoons groundnut oil

butter and jam, to serve

1 Put the buckwheat and plain flour, baking powder and honey in a bowl.

2 Make a well in the centre, add egg and milk and stir to make a thick batter.

3 Oil a frying pan with a spoonful of groundnut oil and leave to get hot and hazy. When the pan is hot pour off the oil into a heatproof bowl or cup and keep it handy.

4 Spoon mixture in tablespoons, one at a time, into the pan. When bubbles rise to the surface, flip the pancake over with a palette knife perhaps and cook on the other side for about 30 seconds. Lift and keep warm by wrapping in a clean tea-towel. Repeat, heating the pan each time, to make 12 pancakes or until all the batter is used up. Serve warm with butter and jam.

• **To save time, the batter can be made the night before and kept in the fridge in a measuring jug. Stir well before using.**

ZESTY FRUIT AND NUT MUFFINS

These muffins are rich in healthy nutrients.

MAKES 12
50 g (2 oz) wheat bran
5 tablespoons natural yogurt
50 g (2 oz) stoned prunes
50 g (2 oz) broken walnuts
3 egg whites
2 tablespoons olive oil
2 tablespoons honey
175 g (6 oz) oat bran
2 teaspoons baking powder
1 teaspoon ground cinnamon
¼ teaspoon ground nutmeg
½ teaspoon ground ginger
2 tablespoons sunflower seeds
50 g (2 oz) raisins
1 tablespoon grated orange rind
1 tablespoon grated lemon rind
sifted icing sugar, to serve

1 Line a 12 muffin pan with paper cases. Preheat the oven to 200C (400F/Gas 6).

2 Mix together the wheat bran and yogurt and set aside. Chop the prunes and walnuts.

3 In a mixing bowl, whisk egg whites until stiff. Fold in the oil and honey and then add the wheat bran mixture.

4 Mix together oat bran, baking powder, cinnamon, nutmeg and ginger. Add to egg mixture and mix together. Stir in chopped prunes, walnuts, sunflower seeds, raisins, grated orange and lemon rinds.

5 Spoon mixture into the cases and bake for 15–20 minutes or until a cocktail stick, inserted in the centre, comes out clean. Serve warm dusted with icing sugar.

• Any muffins not eaten fresh on the day are delicious toasted and buttered the next day.

APRICOT, FIG AND RAISIN BALLS ROLLED IN SESAME SEEDS

Make a large batch of these for a natural healthy booster. They're easy to make and are excellent for breakfasts on the hoof. I eat them to give me a lift before an important meeting, if driving a long distance or when I'm just a little tired and have a busy day ahead of me.

MAKES 14 small balls
50 g (2 oz) figs
50g (2 oz) apricots
50 g (2 oz) raisins
25 g (1 oz) sesame seeds

1 Remove the stalks from the figs then put the figs, apricots and raisins into the bowl of the food processor and whizz until the mixture forms a ball in the bowl. Alternatively, if you have no food processor, with diligence, use a good sharp knife and chop all the fruit until very small. Dip the knife in the flour if the fruit becomes too sticky on the knife's blade.

2 Now form the fruit mixture into small balls, slightly larger than a Malteser and then roll in sesame seeds.

3 Store in an airtight container in a fridge.

• For a great breakfast, put five balls, with a chopped apple and sliced banana, into a bowl with low fat yogurt over the top.

Clockwise from top: *Zesty fruit and nut muffins; Warming hot chocolate; Hot cinnamon toast; Apricot, fig and raisin balls rolled in sesame seeds.*

FRUITY PORRIDGE

No breakfast chapter would be complete without this old fashioned Scottish staple. Traditional Scottish porridge is made with pinhead oatmeal which needs to be soaked as it is very coarse and grainy. I make my porridge with porridge oats which is quite different but equally delicious. I have added a few of my favourite dried fruits to make it interesting and half milk, half water to make it extra creamy.

SERVES 4

50 g (2 oz) dried pears
50 g (2 oz) dried peaches
125 g (4 oz) Scottish porridge oats
500 ml (17 fl oz) milk and water (or all water)
salt, to taste

1 Chop the pears and peaches. Put in a medium saucepan with the oats, milk and water and mix together.

2 Bring to the boil, then simmer for 5 minutes, stirring occasionally. Serve hot.

• If you have a sweet tooth, serve with extra maple syrup and milk.

PEACHY YOGHURT SHAKE

This is a refreshing yogurt drink.

SERVES 4

2 ripe peaches
1 ripe banana
450 ml (¾ pint) natural yogurt
150 ml (¼ pint) apple juice

1 Peel and roughly chop peaches and banana. Put in a blender or food processor, add the yogurt and apple juice and blend together until smooth and frothy. Serve chilled.

• For added texture and extra nutrients, you may like to add a handful of oat bran or sunflower seeds.

WARMING HOT CHOCOLATE

Best of all, I like hot chocolate with a dash of brandy – omit for mornings but definite for night times.

SERVES 2

2 teaspoons cocoa powder
sugar, to taste
300 ml (½ pint) whole or semi-skimmed milk
pinch of cinnamon (optional)
dash of brandy (optional)

1 Put a teaspoonful of cocoa powder into 2 mugs and add sugar to taste. Blend with a little of the milk to form a smooth paste.

2 Bring remaining milk to the boil then pour into the mugs, stirring. Add cinnamon or brandy to taste, if wished.

• Don't be tempted to use drinking chocolate instead of cocoa powder as it is over-sweet. To make it frothy, whizz it in the liquidiser.

BANANA AND HONEY SUPER SHAKE

I first had this Shake in France, where I was ski-ing one Christmas. It was wonderful!

SERVES 4

500 ml (176 fl oz) soya milk, preferably
  unsweetened
2 medium ripe bananas
1 dessertspoon runny honey or maple syrup
generous pinch of ground cinnamon
½ teaspoon natural vanilla essence

1 Put all the ingredients in a blender or food processor and blend until thick and smooth.

2 Pour into glasses and serve immediately.

• Sometimes I put in ice cubes, which makes it thicker and colder. Good with cow's milk too.

HOT APPLE JUICE WITH CINNAMON, LEMON AND CLOVES

This drink makes a refreshing change from tea and coffee in the morning. It is zesty, comforting and healthy too (and great cold).

SERVES 4

3 tablespoons apple juice concentrate (available
  from health food stores)
1 cinnamon stick
6 cloves
grated rind and juice of 1 lemon

1 Put 600 ml (1 pint) water, the apple juice, cinnamon stick, cloves, lemon rind and juice in a medium saucepan and slowly bring to the boil. Cover and simmer for 20 minutes. Strain and serve.

• I suggest that you have a jug of this mixture in the fridge, so that it can be enjoyed at a moments notice. Leave to cool before storing. Reheat when required or serve cold.

ESPRESSO WITH AMARETTO AND CREAM

This is a very special coffee which, in Italy is drunk only in the morning, often on Sundays as a treat.

SERVES 1

4 tablespoons hot, strong espresso coffee
1 tablespoon single cream
1 tablespoon amaretto liqueur
1 slice lemon, to serve
little sugar, if wished

1 Put the coffee, cream, and amaretto in a jug and mix together. Add a little sugar to taste, if wished. Serve in a warmed glass with a slice of lemon on top.

• Other liqueurs such as Cointreau, Tia Maria, Drambuie or Calvados could be used instead of the amaretto. Choose your favourite.

Light
Lunches

*I*n the middle of the day, something light and tasty is usually all that is needed to sustain you. All the recipes in this chapter can be served on their own and many could be served as a starter or a light supper dish. None of these recipes take long to prepare but all are good to eat whether you are at home or at work.

WARM MARINATED MILLET SALAD

Grains are delicious served not only as an accompaniment to a meal but as the base of a salad, as in this recipe.

SERVES 4

225 g (8 oz) millet

2 garlic cloves

2 tablespoons lemon juice

4 teaspoons balsamic vinegar

2 tablespoons extra virgin olive oil

salt and pepper

100 g (4 oz) cucumber

100 g (4 oz) cherry tomatoes

3 tablespoons chopped fresh basil

1 Put millet in a large frying pan and dry roast, stirring frequently, until the millet turns light golden and smells nutty.

2 Now add 600 ml (1 pint) of water, bring to the boil and simmer for 20 minutes until water has been absorbed.

3 Meanwhile, crush the garlic into a bowl and add the lemon juice, vinegar, olive oil, ¼ teaspoon salt and 1 teaspoon pepper. Whisk together until well mixed.

4 Dice the cucumbers. Toss cucumber, tomatoes and basil into marinade and add the warm cooked millet. Mix well and serve at room temperature.

• Sometimes I scent the cooked grain water with garlic or chilli to give the grains an even greater flavour.

MANGE-TOUT, CANNELLINI AND ALMOND SALAD

A salad should excite the eye and I love the colour and textures of this one. The different shapes of ingredients hold the dressing in its contours.

SERVES 4

225 g (8 oz) mange-tout

salt and pepper

1 red onion

50 g (2 oz) flaked almonds

430 g (1 lb) can cannellini beans

2 tablespoons olive oil

2 teaspoons lemon juice

3 tablespoons creme fraiche (optional)

1 Plunge the mange-tout into a pan of boiling salted water for 2 minutes to blanch. Drain and refresh under cold running water. Pat dry and leave to cool.

2 Meanwhile, finely slice the onion. Toast the almonds on a sheet of foil under the grill, turning them frequently. Drain the cannellini beans and rinse.

3 In a small saucepan, gently warm the olive oil over a low heat then add the lemon juice and whisk together. Pour over the mange-tout and mix together. Add the cannellini beans, onion, almonds and creme fraiche if wished. Season well with salt and pepper and serve.

• The flavour of this salad improves with age so, if possible, make it several hours before it is to be needed and serve at room temperature.

CARROT, CHEESE AND PARSLEY SANDWICH WITH MAYO

This sandwich is an old favourite from my very first business. It is colourful and crunchy.

MAKES 2 ROUNDS OF SANDWICHES

2 medium carrots

2 spring onions

1 handful of flat-leaved fresh parsley

2 tablespoons mayonnaise

4 tablespoons grated mature cheese

4 slices of bread, preferably brown or rye

butter, for spreading

1 Grate the carrots. Finely chop the spring onions and parsley. Put the carrots, onions, parsley, mayonnaise and cheese in a bowl and mix together.

2 Spread the slices of bread with butter, spread 2 slices with the filling mixture then top with the remaining bread slices.

• The filling mixture can be kept, covered, in the fridge for up to 2 days.

BEETROOT AND FETA SANDWICH WITH PARSLEY

Beetroot is naturally sweet and delicious and combined with feta cheese makes a good sandwich.

MAKES 2 ROUNDS OF SANDWICHES

handful of fresh parsley

4 slices of wholegrain or rye bread

butter, for spreading

2 medium slices of cooked beetroot

100 g (4 oz) feta cheese

grated rind of 1 lemon

1 Finely chop the parsley. Spread the slices of bread with butter.

2 Put the slices of beetroot on 2 slices of bread, crumble over the feta cheese then sprinkle with the parsley and lemon rind. Top each with the remaining bread slices.

• Make just before serving as the beetroot tends to run and stain the bread.

SUN DRIED TOMATO PESTO AND PICKLED AUBERGINE SANDWICH

This is my all time best-ever sandwich. It's just all my favourite flavours together and I think it's brilliant on good olive bread.

MAKES 2 ROUNDS OF SANDWICHES

butter, for spreading

4 slices of olive bread

2 tablespoons sun dried tomato pesto (see page 137)

2 tablespoons pickled aubergine (see page 136)

4 lollo rosso or Cos lettuce leaves

1 Spread butter on bread. Put pesto, aubergine and lettuce on 2 slices. Top with remaining bread.

• Hunt out a supplier of good bread; buy fresh, cut into slices and freeze what you can't eat in bundles of two. Thaw for 2 hours at room temperature.

BROAD BEANS AND MINT WITH GORGONZOLA DRESSING

I adore broad beans and when they are in season from the end of May to July, this salad is something I really relish. In Italy they are often eaten with goats' or pecorino cheese but this blue cheese dressing is my favourite.

SERVES 4

1.5 kg (3 lb) fresh broad beans in pods

handful of fresh mint

50 g (2 oz) gorgonzola cheese

2-3 tablespoons fruity extra virgin olive oil

2 drops of balsamic vinegar

salt and pepper

1 red onion

crusty bread, to serve

1 Shell the beans. Steam the beans for about 8 minutes, until tender. Plunge into cold water then drain well. Turn into a salad bowl or shallow serving dish.

2 Finely chop the mint. Using a wooden spoon, mix together mint, cheese, oil, balsamic vinegar, salt and pepper and beat to make a dressing.

3 Pour the dressing over the cold broad beans and toss together. Skin and finely chop onion then sprinkle over the top. Serve with crusty bread.

• If you can't get fresh broad beans use frozen ones and take the time to skin them of their tough white outer layer. Inside is a tender, bright green bean that looks and tastes stunning.

BAKED AUBERGINE, OLIVE AND MOZZARELLA SANDWICH WITH BASIL

This is a very good substantial sandwich. It's particularly good in a French loaf.

SERVES 4

1 small aubergine

extra virgin olive oil

100 g (4 oz) stoned black olives

salt and pepper

handful of fresh basil

4 radicchio leaves

1 French loaf

4 slices mozzarella cheese

1 Preheat the oven to 200C (400F/Gas 6). Slice aubergine lengthways, brush with olive oil and place on a baking tray. Bake for 20 minutes, turning once. Remove from the oven and leave to cool.

2 Chop olives until very small and make a creamy paste. Put in a bowl and add some pepper, the torn basil leaves and shredded radicchio leaves and mix together.

3 To assemble the sandwich, cut the French loaf in half lengthways. Arrange a layer of mozzarella cheese on the base and sprinkle on a little salt. Add the aubergine slices, then the radicchio and basil mixture.

4 Top with the bread and serve cut into short lengths.

• This is a wonderful way to cook aubergines and is no more difficult or time-consuming than grilling toast. Once cooked they'll keep for up to 1 day in the fridge.

Clockwise from top: *Broad beans and mint with gorgonzola dressing; Cheesey carrot and nut bites with sesame seeds; Baked aubergine, olive and mozzarella sandwich with basil.*

CHEESEY CARROT AND NUT BITES WITH SESAME SEEDS

These quick savoury balls are great served hot in pitta bread or with a salad.

SERVES 4

½ an onion

handful of fresh parsley

2 medium carrots

225 g (8 oz) salted peanuts

100 g (4 oz) mature Cheddar cheese

225 g (8 oz) fresh breadcrumbs

pinch of dried thyme

1 tablespoon extra virgin olive oil

pepper

sesame seeds, to coat

1 Preheat the oven to 200C (400F/Gas 6). Put all ingredients, except the sesame seeds, in a food processor and blend together until all ingredients are small and have bound together.

2 Form the mixture into even-sized balls then roll in sesame seeds. Bake in the oven for 15 minutes, until golden. (For party nibbles or picnics, roll the mixture into very small balls and bake for 10 minutes, until golden.)

• If you do not have a food processor, grate the carrot and finely chop the other ingredients.

ROASTED TOMATOES ON TOAST WITH GOATS' CHEESE AND CORIANDER

This is one of those recipes where a few simple ingredients marry together into something amazingly tasty. Good bread, good oil, good tomatoes – great toasties!

SERVES 4

4 slices of day old country bread

2 tablespoons fruity extra virgin olive oil

4 ripe tomatoes, preferably Italian plum

handful of fresh coriander

100 g (4 oz) vegetarian goats' cheese

grated rind of ½ a lemon

salt and pepper

1 garlic clove

fresh coriander leaves and chives, to garnish

1 Preheat the oven to 200C (400F/Gas 6). Brush bread on both sides with olive oil. Arrange on a baking tray and bake for 10 minutes, until brown. Cool on a rack.

2 Using the same tray as for the bread, drizzle with a little oil and place the tomatoes on it. Bake at the same temperature for 15 minutes, until the skins are blackened. Leave to cool.

3 Finely chop the coriander. Mix coriander, goats' cheese, lemon rind and juice together. Season with salt and pepper and leave to one side.

4 The tomatoes should now be cool enough to handle. Skin and cut in half, scoop out seeds and chop flesh in even pieces. Drizzle with the remaining oil.

5 Skin the garlic clove and rub over the surface of the toasted bread. Spread on the goats' cheese mixture and top with tomato flesh. Garnish with coriander and chives.

• Try mashed feta cheese instead of the goats' and top with Greek black olives.

WARM CREAMY COURGETTE, CORIANDER AND SPINACH TOASTS

This makes a light, fresh, good-for-you lunch.

SERVES 4

225 g (8 oz) young, tender courgettes

1 garlic clove

225 g (8 oz) tender spinach

50 g (2 oz) fresh coriander leaves

50 g (2 oz) butter

salt and pepper

pinch of freshly grated nutmeg

2 tablespoons creme fraiche or mascarpone

4 slices of bread

extra virgin olive oil, for brushing

1 Slice the courgettes. Chop the garlic. Wash and chop the spinach. Chop the coriander, reserving a few leaves to garnish.

2 Heat the butter in a large frying pan, add the courgettes and cook for 5 minutes, stirring often. Add a touch of salt to extract the courgette juices. Now add the garlic and spinach, with some of the water still clinging to the leaves after washing, cover and cook for a further 5 minutes, stirring occasionally. Leave to cool for 5 minutes.

3 Put the vegetables into a food processor with the chopped coriander, nutmeg, salt and pepper. Blend together. Add the cream cheese and blend again.

4 To serve, toast the bread slices on both sides then brush with the extra virgin olive oil. Gently warm the creamy vegetable mixture and serve on the toast, garnished with the reserved coriander leaves.

• Coriander is my favourite herb and I try to buy it in a bunch with roots on. To keep it fresh, fill a jug with cold water, plunge the stalks into it as you wold a bunch of flowers in a vase, cover with a poly bag and keep in the fridge. Check daily and remove any yellow leaves. It'll keep fresh for up to 1 week.

BEAN SPROUT SALAD WITH NUTS, APPLE AND RAISINS

In my first job after leaving college, I used to make this salad for a small coffee shop. I have fond memories of picking the bean sprouts up first thing in the morning, freshly grown by a Chinese family. They would then be made into this quick salad that's really crunchy.

SERVES 4

50 g (2 oz) raisins

450 g (1 lb) fresh bean sprouts

1 eating apple

75 g (3 oz) salted peanuts

75 g (3 oz) mayonnaise

pepper

1 Put the raisins in a bowl, pour over hot water and leave to soak for 20 minutes, until plump. Drain and discard the water.

2 Wash and dry the bean sprouts well and put in a bowl. Core the apple, chop into small chunks and add to the sprouts. Add the raisins, peanuts, mayonnaise and pepper and mix well together.

• You may like to grow your own sprouts at home using alfalfa or mung beans and chick peas.

ROASTED RED PEPPER, CREAM CHEESE AND ROCKET OPEN SANDWICHES

The contrast of the sweet pepper and cheese, with the pepperiness of the rocket, goes so well in this colourful bread topping. It is particularly good on foccacia bread.

MAKES 8 SMALL SANDWICHES
1 red pepper
100 g (4 oz) cream cheese
salt and pepper
4 slices of bread, such as foccacia
handful of rocket

1 Preheat the oven to 200C (400F/Gas 6). Put the pepper on a baking tray and roast in the oven for 20 minutes, until deflated and slightly charred, turning once during cooking. Leave to cool then peel off the skin.

2 Chop the pepper flesh, discarding the core and seeds, and put in a bowl. Add the cheese, season with salt and pepper and mix together.

3 To assemble the sandwiches, spread the roasted pepper cheese generously on the slices of bread, cut each slice in half then top with rocket.

• When skinning the pepper, hold it over a bowl to collect the precious juices. These can then be kept and used for salad dressings.

FRIED MOZZARELLA SANDWICHES

In Italy these are known as Mozzarella in Carrozza, which means Mozzarella in a Carriage. These were my Grandfather's favourite snack.

MAKES 4 SANDWICHES
4 thick slices of bread
175 g (6 oz) Mozzarella cheese
handful of torn fresh basil
salt and pepper
2 tablespoons milk
flour, for dusting
2 eggs
125 ml (4 fl oz) olive oil

1 Cut the bread slices in half to give 8 slices. Thinly slice the cheese then sandwich between the bread slices, adding torn basil leaves and salt and pepper to taste.

2 Now sprinkle the sandwiches with milk and dip in flour.

3 Beat together the eggs then allow the sandwiches to soak in the beaten eggs.

4 Press the edges to enclose the cheese and basil securely.

5 Heat the oil in the frying pan and fry sandwiches on both sides until golden. Drain on absorbent kitchen paper. Serve at once.

• A host of different fillings can be used to accompany the mozzarella – I like black olives – but try sun-dried tomatoes, a good layer of chopped fresh parsley or some capers.

Top to bottom: *Roasted red pepper, cream cheese and rocket open sandwiches; Tomato and mint salad; Fried mozzarella sandwiches.*

TOMATO AND MINT SALAD

This salad is simple, tasty and colourful.

SERVES 4
4 firm, bright red tomatoes
½ a small red onion
handful of fresh mint
3 tablespoons extra virgin olive oil
salt and pepper
shavings of Parmesan cheese
crusty bread, to serve

1 Slice tomatoes and arrange on a large plain plate. Finely chop the onion and mint and sprinkle over the tomatoes. Dress with olive oil, salt and pepper.

2 Serve with shaving of Parmesan and crusty bread.

• To select the best tomatoes, smell their stalk end. The should have a strong peppery aroma. Buy tomatoes that have been sun-ripened outdoors for the best flavour.

MUSHROOM CROSTINI WITH LEEKS AND ARTICHOKES

Marinate mushrooms in a lemon dressing, serve on toast and top with leeks, artichokes and peppers for a most delicious snack.

SERVES 4
8 slices of day old open textured bread
3 tablespoons olive oil
3 young, tender leeks
4 flat mushrooms
4 cooked artichoke hearts
grated rind and juice of 1 lemon
salt and pepper
drop of balsamic vinegar
1 red pepper
1 garlic clove
8 basil leaves, to garnish

1 Preheat the oven to 200C (400F/Gas 6). Put the bread slices on a baking tray, brush with a little oil and bake in the oven for 12–14 minutes, until golden. Leave to cool.

2 Meanwhile, slice the leeks and wash well under cold running water. Slice the mushrooms and chop the artichoke hearts into small pieces. Heat 1 tablespoon oil in a frying pan and saute the leeks, mushrooms and artichoke hearts for about 15 minutes until tender. Put in a bowl and pour over remaining olive oil, lemon rind and juice, salt and pepper and balsamic vinegar. Leave for 2 to 3 hours or even overnight, to allow the flavours to infuse, stirring occasionally.

3 Meanwhile, put the pepper on a baking tray and roast at 200C (400F/Gas 6) for 20 minutes, until deflated and slightly blackened. Leave to cool then, holding the pepper over the marinating vegetables, peel off the skin, allowing the juices to run into the vegetables. Cut the flesh into strips, discarding the core and seeds.

4 Now skin the garlic and rub the clove over the toasted bread to impart its flavour.

5 To serve, spoon mushroom mixture over toast, place a piece of roasted pepper on top and garnish with a basil leaf.

• To save time, leave the vegetables to marinate in their lemon dressing overnight.

ROCKET AND ALMOND PESTO ON RYE TOASTS

Rocket has become increasingly popular over the last few years. It has a delicious sharp peppery flavour. It can be grown very easily and makes an excellent salad leaf. I hope you will agree that this pesto sauce makes a change from the conventional basil variety.

SERVES 4

4 slices of rye bread

3 tablespoons extra virgin olive oil

Pesto

2 tablespoons freshly grated pecorino cheese plus shavings, to garnish

very large handful of rocket leaves

1 small garlic clove

grated rind of ½ a lemon plus ½ a lemon, to garnish

12 whole almonds

4 sun dried tomatoes in oil

salt and pepper

1 Toast the rye bread and, with a pastry brush, brush on some olive oil to dampen the surface of the toast.

2 Put the cheese in a food processor bowl. Add the rocket leaves, reserving 4 small leaves to garnish, the garlic, grated lemon rind, almonds, remaining oil, tomatoes and salt and pepper and blend together to make a thick pesto sauce.

3 To serve, spread the pesto sauce generously on to the slices of rye bread. Using a canelle knife, pare the rind from the lemon half then tie 4 strips into a knot. Use to garnish the toast, together with a few shavings of pecorino cheese and the reserved small rocket leaves.

• If you don't have a canelle knife to remove the rind from the lemon, use a potato peeler and cut the rind into thin strips with a sharp knife.

ROASTED GARLIC AND DOLCELATTE TOASTS

This recipe is very quick and very tasty. It uses a whole garlic bulb which, when roasted, is surprisingly sweet and mild.

SERVES 4

4 slices of open textured bread

2 tablespoons extra virgin olive oil

1 whole garlic bulb

100 g (4 oz) dolcelatte cheese

fresh dill, to garnish

1 Preheat the oven to 200C (400F/Gas 6). Put the bread slices on a baking tray, brush with oil then bake in the oven, with the whole garlic bulb, for 15 minutes, turning the bread over after 7 minutes.

2 Squeeze the garlic cloves individually from the papery skin and now press all the soft garlic flesh through a sieve. You should have a soft, golden puree.

3 Now mix the garlic puree and dolcelatte cheese together until creamy. Spread on to the toasts and serve garnished with dill.

• Dolcelatte cheese is mild and creamy but other semi-soft blue-veined cheeses such as Gorgonzola and mycella can be used.

BITTER LEAVES WITH ROMESCO DRESSING

This salad has a wonderful pink dressing.

SERVES 4
Dressing
8 almonds
12 hazelnuts
4 tomatoes
1 garlic clove
6 tablespoons good fruity extra virgin olive oil
1 tablespoon day old breadcrumbs
1 teaspoon sweet paprika
2½ teaspoons red wine vinegar
handful of flat-leaved fresh parsley
pinch of cayenne pepper
salt and pepper
Salad
1 frisee
bunch of rocket
1 chicory head
handful of green olives
handful of black olives

1 First make the dressing. Preheat the oven to 190C (375F/Gas 5). Put the almonds and hazelnuts on a baking tray and toast in the oven for 20 minutes, turning occasionally.

2 Put the tomatoes in a bowl, cover with boiling water for about 30 seconds then plunge into cold water. Peel off the skins then chop the flesh.

3 Cut garlic into slivers. Heat 1 tablespoon oil in a frying pan, add garlic and fry until golden. Transfer to a processor.

4 Fry the breadcrumbs in remaining oil in the pan. Sprinkle with paprika.

5 Add the toasted nuts to the garlic and blend until the nuts are ground adding the chopped tomatoes, vinegar, parsley and 5 tablespoons of oil. Mix in the breadcrumbs and cayenne. Season with salt and pepper.

6 Put the frisee, rocket and chicory leaves in a large bowl. Add dressing and toss. Garnish with olives.

• **The dressing is very versatile and is great on green beans or broccoli.**

PICKLED RED ONION AND AVOCADO OPEN SANDWICHES

This simple combination works so well. I love the two colours together.

MAKES 4 OPEN SANDWICHES
2 tablespoons pickled red onion (see page 134)
   or 1 fresh red onion
1 avocado, preferably hass
4 slices of bread
butter, for spreading
dash of balsamic vinegar
salt and pepper

1 If using a fresh onion, skin and finely chop. Peel and slice the avocado. Spread the slices of bread with butter.

2 To assemble the sandwiches, arrange the avocado slices on the slices of bread. Add the vinegar and season with salt and pepper to taste. Top each with 1 tablespoon pickled red onion or the chopped raw onion. Serve immediately.

• **To ripen an avocado, place in a brown bag, with a banana.**

Clockwise from top: *Bitter leaves with romesco dressing; Pickled red cabbage and avocado open sandwiches; Baked potato with tomato, hazelnut and thyme filling.*

BAKED POTATOES

To make the potatoes crispy, I brush the outsides with oil and sprinkle with salt.

medium baking potatoes, such as Pentland Squire

olive oil

sea salt

1 Preheat the oven to 200C (400F/Gas 6). Scrub the potatoes well, until clean. Dry and toss in olive oil, then sprinkle with salt.

2 Bake in the oven for 1–1½ hours, until tender right through.

• I like to use Pentland Squire potatoes for baking but other good varieties include Marie Piper, Estima, Cara and King Edward.

TOMATO, HAZELNUT AND THYME FILLING

A colourful and tasty combination.

SERVES 4

4 medium baking potatoes

100 g (4 oz) hazelnuts

4 tomatoes

handful of fresh thyme

175 g (6 oz) dolcelatte cheese

salt and pepper

1 Prepare and bake the potatoes as described above.

2 Toast the hazelnuts on a sheet of foil under the grill, stirring, then chop.

3 Put the tomatoes in a bowl, cover with boiling water for about 30 seconds then plunge into cold water. Peel off the skins then chop the flesh, discarding the seeds.

4 Reserve a few sprigs of thyme to garnish then chop the thyme, discarding the stems.

5 Put the hazelnuts, tomatoes, thyme, dolcelatte, salt and pepper in a bowl and mix together.

6 When the potatoes are cooked, slash them and stuff with the filling. Garnish with the reserved sprigs of thyme.

• Buy nuts in small amounts from a supplier with a good turnover to enjoy them at their freshest. You can revive any you find at the back of your cupboard by toasting them and using them straight away.

POPPY SEED, CELERY, GORGONZOLA AND CHIVE FILLING

This is a lovely creamy filling.

SERVES 4

4 medium baking potatoes

2 celery sticks

175 g (6 oz) gorgonzola cheese

1 dessertspoon poppy seeds

handful of chopped fresh chives

1 Prepare and bake potatoes as above.

2 Finely chop the celery sticks. Put the celery, cheese, poppy seeds and chives in a bowl and mix together with a fork to make a thick cream.

3 When the potatoes are cooked, slash them and stuff with the filling.

• Black poppy seeds are most widely available but you can also buy white poppy seeds. Either are suitable and they add a wonderful crunchy texture and nutty flavour.

CELERIAC AND PECORINO FILLING

Celeriac has a beautiful pungent flavour and combines deliciously with potato.

SERVES 4

4 medium baking potatoes

450 g (1 lb) celeriac

100 g (4 oz) pecorino cheese

a little butter

salt and pepper

chopped fresh chervil, to garnish

shavings of pecorino cheese, to garnish
(optional)

1 Prepare and bake potatoes as on page 32.

2 Peel the celeriac and chop into even sized 25 cm (1 in) pieces then steam for 9 minutes until tender.

3 Meanwhile, grate the cheese. Mash the cooked celeriac in a bowl then add the cheese, butter, salt and pepper. Stir well.

4 Use filling to stuff potatoes. Garnish with chervil and pecorino cheese if wished.

• Celeriac goes brown once the cut surfaces are exposed to the air so unless you are going to cook it immediately, put it into cold water with a little lemon juice added.

CABBAGE, MUSHROOM AND EGG FILLING

The combination of dill, mushrooms, cabbage, cream cheese and eggs is really tasty.

SERVES 4

4 medium baking potatoes

225 g (8 oz) white cabbage

100 g (4 oz) flat mushrooms

2 spring onions

2 eggs, hard-boiled

2 tablespoons olive oil

175 g (6 oz) cream cheese

handful of fresh or 2 teaspoons dried dill

salt and pepper

1 Prepare and bake potatoes as on page 32.

2 Finely shred the cabbage. Roughly chop the mushrooms. Chop the spring onions. Slice the hard-boiled eggs.

3 Heat a frying pan, add oil and cabbage and stir-fry. Add mushrooms, spring onions, salt and pepper and fry until tender.

4 Transfer the vegetables to a bowl, add eggs, cheese, dill, salt and pepper and stir well. Use to stuff potatoes.

• Use garlic instead of spring onions.

ROASTED RED PEPPER AND SPINACH FILLING

SERVES 4

4 medium baking potatoes

2 medium red peppers

500 g (1 lb) tender young spinach

50 g (2 oz) freshly grated Parmesan cheese

salt and pepper

1 Prepare and bake potatoes as on page 32.

2 Roast peppers for 25 minutes. Cool, peel and chop. Wash spinach and cook for 5 minutes. Drain, chop and add peppers, cheese, salt and pepper. Use to stuff potatoes.

• The peppers and spinach can be prepared in advance and reheated. Add the Parmesan cheese just before serving.

Midweek Meals

During the week we are often short of time, tired and hungry at the end of the day. This is when we are in need of something that's quick to cook, something that's ready to sit down to in half an hour. Turn the page and share some of my most-trusted mid-week meals.

FENNEL UNDER A GARLIC CHEESE CRUMB

This dish can be served as a starter, in individual ramekins, or as a side vegetable. Fennel is an extremely tasty vegetable. It is often eaten raw after a meal as a digestive.

SERVES 6

2 male fennel heads (see tip •)

1 whole garlic bulb

200 g (8 oz) dolcelatte cheese

50 ml (2 fl oz) single cream

salt and pepper

100 g (4 oz) toasted breadcrumbs (see tip •)

1 Preheat the oven to 200C (400F/Gas 6). Trim the fennel and wash well. Cut into even lengths and steam for 12 minutes, until tender.

2 Put the whole garlic bulb on a baking tray and bake in the oven for 20 minutes, until soft. Remove the papery layers from the garlic bulb, leaving the soft garlic cloves. Push the cloves through a sieve to obtain a puree.

3 Chop the cheese and put in a bowl. Add the garlic puree, cream, salt and pepper and mix well. Taste and adjust seasoning if you feel it needs more salt or pepper.

4 Either butter an ovenproof serving dish or 6 ramekin dishes then put in a layer of fennel and then a layer of the cheese mixture. Repeat these layers then finish with toasted breadcrumbs.

5 Bake in the oven at 200C (400F/Gas 6) for 20 minutes until crisp and bubbling.

• **The male fennel is long and thin and the female fennel is bulbous – almost as if it has hips. The male has more flavour. To make toasted breadcrumbs, spread on a baking tray and toast at 200C (400F/ Gas 6) for about 7 minutes, stirring once.**

VEGETABLE STOCK

Vegetable stock is so easy to make and it adds your own hallmark of flavour to soups, rather than relying on commercial stock cubes. I recommend that you keep your vegetable peelings for over a period of 2-3 days, until you have a substantial amount of clean peelings.

2 tablespoons olive oil

carrot peelings

potato peelings

celeriac peelings

celery stalks, broccoli stalks, cabbage leaves etc.

small amount of onion skins

garlic skins

handful of fresh parsley

2 bay leaves

salt and pepper

1 Heat the oil in a large saucepan. When the pan is hot, add all the clean peelings and stir-fry in the oil, until the peelings have wilted.

2 Add 1 litre (32 fl oz) water, vegetables, vegetable skins, parsley and bay leaves. Bring to the boil then simmer for 40 minutes.

3 Strain the stock and use or store in the fridge for up to 2 days. Season before using.

• **Make a big pan of stock and freeze it in handy qunatities. To save space in your freezer, reduce it by boiling rapidly in an uncovered saucepan to make a concentrated stock with an intense flavour. Don't add salt or pepper until you are ready to use it.**

ARTICHOKE, LEMON AND ALMOND SOUP

Although perhaps unusual, the combination of these ingredients, I think, is rather excellent. It is smooth, with a fresh flavour.

SERVES 4

½ an onion

1 garlic clove

100 g (3½ oz) ground almonds

4 tablespoons olive oil

salt and pepper

6 cooked baby artichoke hearts

1 litre (32 fl oz) vegetable stock (see page 36)

juice of 1 lemon

dash of white wine vinegar

pinch of sugar

snipped fresh chives, to garnish

crusty bread, to serve

1 Chop the onion. Crush the garlic. Toast the almonds on a sheet of foil under the grill, stirring frequently.

2 In a large saucepan, fry the onion in 1 tablespoon of olive oil, adding salt to draw out the juices. When the onion has softened, add the crushed garlic, almonds, remaining oil, artichokes, stock, lemon juice, vinegar, sugar and pepper. Bring to the boil and then simmer for 20 minutes.

3 Allow to cool down then blend well in a food processor.

4 Adjust seasoning, garnish with chives and serve with crusty bread.

• If unable to find fresh artichoke hearts, use canned.

TANGY TOMATO SOUP WITH LEMON GRASS

This soup is impressive yet easy to make.

SERVES 6

1 kg (2 lb) fresh ripe tomatoes

1.2 litres (2 pints) vegetable stock (see page 36)

1 fresh lemon grass stalk or grated lemon rind

1 small chilli

1½ teaspoons sea salt

2 teaspoons sugar

1 tablespoon lemon juice

2 tablespoons finely chopped spring onions

1 tablespoon chopped fresh coriander

2 teaspoons sun dried tomato puree (see tip •)

2 teaspoons sesame oil

fresh coriander leaves, to garnish

1 Put the tomatoes in a bowl, cover with boiling water for about 30 seconds then plunge into cold water. Using a sharp knife, peel off the skins then cut the flesh into cubes, discarding the seeds.

2 Put the stock in a saucepan and bring to simmering point.

3 Peel the lemon grass stalk to the tender white centre then chop finely. Slice the chilli (see tip •).

4 Add the lemon grass, chilli, salt, sugar, lemon juice, spring onions, coriander and tomato puree to the simmering stock and stir to mix well. Add chopped tomatoes and simmer for 3 minutes, then finally add the sesame oil.

5 Serve hot, garnished with coriander leaves.

• Treat chillies with care as the oils in their flesh can make your skin tingle. Wash your hands thoroughly after preparing them and never allow chillies near your eyes. Discard the seeds if you do not want a very hot flavour.

RICE NOODLE CLOUD WITH STIR-FRIED VEGETABLES

A colourful, aromatic dish with flavours of the Far East.

SERVES 4

300 ml (10 fl oz) groundnut oil

175 g (6 oz) rice noodles (rice vermicelli)

350 g (12 oz) aubergines

225 g (8 oz) courgettes

salt

1 red pepper

1 yellow pepper

4 spring onions

2 garlic cloves

2 tablespoons rice wine

2 tablespoons yellow bean sauce

2 teaspoons chilli bean sauce

150 ml (5 fl oz) vegetable stock (see page 36)

1 teaspoon sugar

2 tablespoons tamari

1 teaspoon cornflour

1 Heat the oil in a wok or large pan until hot. Fry noodles until crisp and puffed up. Drain on kitchen paper.

2 Cut the aubergine and courgettes into 75 cm (3 in) lengths. Sprinkle with salt and leave in a sieve to drain for 20 minutes. Rinse under cold running water and pat dry with kitchen paper.

3 Finely chop the red and yellow pepper, discarding the core and seeds. Chop the onions and crush the garlic. Heat wok or frying pan and add 1½ tablespoons of the oil in which you have fried the noodles. When moderately hot add the spring onions and garlic and stir-fry. Add aubergines, courgettes, red and yellow peppers and fry for 1 minute.

4 Stir in the rice wine, yellow and chilli bean sauces, stock, sugar, tamari and 1 teaspoon salt and cook for 3 minutes. Blend the cornflour with 1 teaspoon water, add to the pan and cook for 1 minute. Put the fried noodles on a warmed platter and spoon the vegetables over the top. Serve straight away.

• Tamari is a sauce made from naturally fermented soya beans. It can be difficult to find but most health food shops and Oriental supermarkets stock it.

BAKED SHALLOTS WITH CREAMY BROCCOLI

SERVES 4

4 shallots

225 g (8 oz) tiny broccoli florets

50 g (2 oz) flaked almonds

100 g (4 oz) cream cheese

salt and pepper

1 Preheat the oven to 190C (375F/Gas 5). Bake the shallots in their skins, in the oven for 25 minutes or until they feel soft when gently squeezed.

2 Meanwhile steam the broccoli florets for 4 minutes or until tender.

3 Toast the almonds on a sheet of foil under the grill, turning them frequently. Mix together the broccoli, almonds, cream cheese, salt and pepper in a bowl.

4 When the shallots are cooked, peel back their skins. Cut in half, add filling then replace the tops of the shallots. Serve warm.

• Use small red onions if shallots are not around.

Top to bottom: *Tangy tomato soup with lemon grass; Rice noodle cloud with stir-fried vegetables; Deep fried risotto with shallots, orange rind and mozzarella.*

Deep fried risotto with shallots, orange rind and mozzarella

I first enjoyed these in Sicily where they are called Orangina meaning little oranges. The risotto is rolled into balls, breadcrumbs and fried. They are very unusual and tasty too.

SERVES 4
1 shallot
handful of mixed fresh herbs
800 ml (27 fl oz) vegetable stock (see page 36)
50 g (2 oz) unsalted butter
275 g (10 oz) arborio (risotto) rice
175 g (6 oz) mozzarella cheese
grated rind of 1 large orange
6 tablespoons freshly grated Parmesan cheese
salt and pepper
1 egg
50 g (2 oz) fresh breadcrumbs
6 tablespoons olive oil

1 Finely chop the shallot. Chop the herbs.

In a saucepan, bring the stock to the boil and keep just below simmering point.

2 Melt the butter in a large saucepan, add rice and brown for a few minutes. Stir in a ladleful of stock and cook until the liquid has been absorbed, stirring constantly until rice is cooked and the liquid has evaporated – this will take about 20 minutes.

3 Grate or cube the mozzarella cheese. Now add cheese, shallot, herbs, orange rind, Parmesan cheese, salt and pepper. Leave to cool then form into balls the size of a plum.

4 Beat the egg and dip the rice balls first into egg and then breadcrumbs.

5 Heat oil in a frying pan and fry rice balls until golden. Drain and serve hot or cold.

• These can be made and coated the day before you are going to serve them.

Chicory rolls

I love chicory cooked, as in this recipe, or raw and crunchy in salads. It has a delicate flavour and makes an unusual dish.

SERVES 4
2 red peppers
4 medium chicory heads
25 g (1 oz) butter
25 g (1 oz) plain white flour
300 ml (½ pint) milk
grated rind and juice of ½ a lemon
1 tablespoon chopped fresh parsley
salt and pepper
25 g (1 oz) mature Cheddar cheese
sprinkling of poppy seeds

1 Preheat the oven to 200C (400F/Gas 6). Put the whole pepper on a baking tray and roast for 20 minutes, until slightly blackened and deflated, turning once during cooking. Leave to cool, then remove skin.

2 Remove any damaged leaves and trim the base from each chicory head. Using a sharp pointed knife, scoop out the hard core. Steam for 10–12 minutes, until tender.

3 Melt the butter in a saucepan. Stir in the flour and cook the roux for 1–2 minutes, stirring. Remove the pan from the heat and, using a wooden spoon, gradually beat in

• Fresh chicory has white leaves with slightly yellow edges. If the leaves are turning green it means that they are not so fresh and will taste bitter.

the milk. Return to the heat and slowly bring to the boil, beating all the time until the sauce boils and thickens. Add the lemon rind and juice and cook for 1 minute. Add the chopped parsley, salt and pepper.

4 Wrap the peeled peppers around the cooked chicory heads. Pack them close together in a 900 ml (1½ pint) ovenproof dish. Spoon the sauce over the top and sprinkle with the cheese and poppy seeds.

5 Place under a preheated grill until golden brown. Serve hot.

ROASTED CHERRY TOMATOES WITH RED ONIONS, SPINACH AND CHEESE SAUCE

This is a real feast on toast! Toasted bread, roasted vegetables, spinach wilted with garlic and a creamy cheese sauce – delicious. I like to serve it with a green salad.

SERVES 4

4 large slices of open textured bread (can be a
  day old)

3 tablespoons olive oil

4 small red onions (as small as possible)

20 cherry tomatoes

Sauce

40 g (1½ oz) butter

25 g (1 oz) plain white flour

300 ml (½ pint) milk

100 g (4 oz) mature Cheddar cheese

salt and pepper

900 g (2 lb) young tender spinach leaves

1 garlic clove

pinch of paprika

1 Preheat the oven to 180C (350F/Gas 4). Brush the slices of bread with some of the olive oil and place on a baking tray. Bake in the oven for 20 minutes until golden, turning after 10 minutes.

2 Remove the outer papery layers of the onions and cook the onions in the oven for about 20 minutes, depending on their size.

The onions should be only just soft.

3 Place the cherry tomatoes in a roasting tin, brush with the remaining oil and place in oven, with the bread and onions.

4 Now make the sauce. In a saucepan, heat the butter until melted, add the flour and cook the roux for 3 minutes, stirring. Remove the pan from the heat and gradually beat in the milk. Return to the heat and slowly bring to the boil, beating all the time, until the sauce boils and thickens. Stir in the cheese, salt and pepper.

5 Wash the spinach well and put in a saucepan with just the water that clings to it after rinsing. Cook for 2 minutes until wilted. Immediately remove spinach from pan and leave to cool.

6 Slice the cooked onions into rings. Skin the garlic clove. Place the toast on individual plates and rub with the garlic clove. Place the tomatoes on the toast, top with spinach leaves and onion rings.

7 Spoon over the cheese sauce. Sprinkle a pinch of paprika on top and bake in the oven for 10 minutes.

• When making a sauce with a roux, always use a wooden spoon as you will get a shinier sauce with a good creamy colour.

Clockwise from top:
*Risotto with
asparagus and peas;
Giant stuffed
mushrooms with pine
nuts and sage; Bread
gnocchi with
rosemary and chervil.*

GIANT STUFFED MUSHROOMS WITH PINE NUTS AND SAGE

Serve on squares of garlic-buttered toast. These look appealing and are very tasty.

SERVES 4

4 very large flat mushrooms

1 small onion

2 celery sticks

1 garlic clove

25 g (1 oz) butter

salt and pepper

25 g (1 oz) pine nuts

75 g (3 oz) cream cheese

1 egg yolk

1 teaspoon chopped fresh sage plus leaves, to
   garnish

25 g (1 oz) wholemeal breadcrumbs

tomato curls (see tip •), to garnish

1 Remove the stalks from the mushrooms and chop finely. Finely chop the onion and the celery. Crush the garlic.

2 Heat the butter in a frying pan, add the onion, cover and cook gently, until soft. Add the celery, mushroom stalks, garlic and season well with salt and pepper. Stir well and simmer, covered, for 10 minutes. Add the pine nuts.

3 Preheat the oven to 180C (350F/Gas 4). In a bowl, cream the cheese. Add the egg yolk and chopped sage and stir in the celery mixture and cheese.

4 Use the cheese mixture to fill the mushroom caps. Arrange on a baking tray and bake in the oven for 20 minutes. Serve, garnished with sage and tomato curls.

• To make tomato curls, use a firm tomato and, with a potato peeler or sharp knife, peel off the skin in one continuous strip.

BREAD GNOCCHI WITH ROSEMARY AND CHERVIL

A simple recipe for a busy lifestyle.

SERVES 4

450 g (1 lb) day old coarse texture loaf

1 litre (1¾ pints) milk

1 shallot

2 teaspoons fresh rosemary

3 teaspoons chervil or fresh parsley

pinch of freshly grated nutmeg

salt and pepper

4 eggs

2 litres (3½ pints) vegetable stock (see page 36)

90 g (3 oz) unsalted butter

50 g (2 oz) freshly grated Parmesan cheese

1 Cut up the bread, discarding crusts, and put in a bowl with the milk. Leave to soak.

2 Meanwhile, finely chop the shallot, rosemary and parsley. When the bread has absorbed the milk, drain, squeeze and put in a bowl. Add the shallot, rosemary, parsley, nutmeg, salt and pepper.

3 Beat the eggs in a bowl and add salt. Now add to the bread and mix to form *firm* dough.

4 Bring the vegetable stock to the boil.

• After soaking the bread, strain the excess milk and use it in a white sauce – it's a shame to waste it.

Form the mixture into balls the size of large chestnuts and drop into the stock. Cover the pan and simmer for 10 minutes. Remove with a slotted spoon. Arrange on a warmed serving dish and keep warm.

5 Set the grill to high. Melt the butter and drizzle over the gnocchi. Sprinkle with Parmesan cheese and cook under the grill for 2 to 3 minutes until the tops are golden brown.

RISOTTO WITH ASPARAGUS, BASIL AND PEAS

You need time and patience to make a risotto although it is not difficult. This version sums up summer for me, when the fresh vegetables are in season. Enjoy it at the rest of the year with the frozen varieties.

SERVES 4
700 g (1½ lb) fresh or 350 g (12 oz) frozen peas
salt and pepper
700 g (1½ lb) young fresh asparagus
about 1.6 litres (2¾ pints) vegetable stock (see
  page 36)
1 medium onion or shallot
100 g (4 oz) unsalted butter
2 tablespoons olive oil
350 g (12 oz) arborio (risotto) rice
1 wine glass of dry white wine
2 tablespoons fresh basil leaves
150 g (5 oz) freshly grated Parmesan cheese
freshly grated Parmesan cheese, to serve

1 Shell the peas. Simmer the fresh peas in boiling salted water for 5 minutes. Drain, refresh in cold water then drain again and set aside.

2 Scrape or shave the asparagus stalks then simmer in boiling, salted water for 3 minutes. Drain and refresh in cold water

then drain again. Finally slice the stalks and set aside.

3 Bring the stock to the boil and keep just below simmering point.

4 Finely chop the onion. Melt half the butter with the oil in a heavy-bottomed saucepan and gently fry the onion, until translucent and soft, then add the rice and cook for a few minutes.

5 Add the white wine and cook until it has evaporated, then add a ladleful of stock and cook until the liquid has been absorbed. Continue adding the stock, stirring between each addition, until the rice is tender but firm. This will take 20–30 minutes, depending on how well cooked you like the rice. When the rice is nearly cooked, add the sliced asparagus, fresh or frozen peas, basil, the remaining butter and the Parmesan cheese.

6 Season with salt and pepper, remove from the heat, stir gently and cover. Leave to stand for about 5 minutes. Stir well before serving with more freshly grated Parmesan cheese.

• To tell if peas are fresh snap a pod. If it breaks crisply and the pod is moist and green they are fresh. If you give them a shake and can hear the peas rattle inside their pods then they are old. Don't buy them.

BAKED BABY PEPPERS

This recipe for stuffed peppers was given to me by my friends in Apulia, Southern Italy.

SERVES 4

8 baby red peppers

2 tablespoons small capers

2 garlic cloves

40 g (1½ oz) coarse, fresh white breadcrumbs

2 large handfuls of chopped flat-leaved fresh parsley

1 handful of chopped fresh mint

3 tablespoons freshly grated pecorino cheese

salt and pepper

225 ml (8 fl oz) dry white wine

4 tablespoons olive oil

bread, to serve

1 Preheat the oven to 200C (400F/Gas 6). Grease a shallow, ovenproof dish.

2 Cut the peppers in half lengthways, discarding the core and seeds. Rinse and chop the capers. Crush the garlic.

3 Arrange the pepper halves in the prepared dish, skin-side down, closely packed in a single layer. Sprinkle over the bread-crumbs, capers, garlic, parsley, mint, cheese, salt and pepper.

4 Spoon over the wine, then drizzle the oil over the peppers. Cover with foil and bake for 30 minutes.

5 Remove foil, return dish to oven and bake for a further 30 minutes or until surface is charred. Leave to cool for 15 minutes, then serve with bread.

• If you are unable to obtain baby peppers use 4 medium peppers and cut into quarters. Have a look at your red pepper. If it has three bumps on the base it is male – four bumps and it is female.

PENNE WITH PUMPKIN AND PECORINO

This recipe uses pumpkin flesh which is cooked in olive oil and garlic then tossed in fresh pasta.

SERVES 4

450 g (1 lb) pumpkin flesh

2 small garlic cloves

handful of flat-leaved fresh parsley

2 tablespoons olive oil

salt and pepper

450 g (1 lb) penne or other tubular cut pasta

3 tablespoons freshly grated pecorino cheese plus extra, to garnish

1 Chop the pumpkin flesh into very small pieces, discarding seeds. Crush garlic. Chop parsley. In a pan heat 1 tablespoon oil, add pumpkin and fry until brown.

2 Add crushed garlic and 300 ml (½ pint) water, salt and pepper. Place lid on the pan and simmer gently for 20–25 minutes, until the pumpkin flesh is soft like a puree.

3 Meanwhile, cook pasta in plenty of boiling, salted water for about 10 minutes until al dente, firm to the bite.

4 When pumpkin is cooked, mix in the remaining 1 tablespoon oil, the parsley, reserving a little to garnish, and the cheese.

5 Drain the cooked pasta and add the pumpkin mixture then mix well. Serve immediately, garnished with the reserved parsley and the cheese.

• As pumpkins are very large you may be able to buy it in slices. If you do need to store a whole pumpkin, keep it in a cool airy place. Store cut pumpkin in a polythene bag in the salad drawer of the refrigerator.

Top to bottom: *Baked baby peppers; Penne with pumpkin and pecorino.*

POTATO CROQUETTES

Creamy mashed potato, rich with butter, cheese and eggs are great served with seasonal vegetables for a satisfying meal.

SERVES 4

1 kg (2 lb) potatoes
3 eggs
40 g (1½ oz) butter
75 g (3 oz) freshly grated Parmesan cheese
salt and pepper
pinch of freshly grated nutmeg
60 g (2¼ oz) fresh wholemeal or white
　breadcrumbs
olive oil, for frying

1 Peel, cut the potatoes into pieces then cook in boiling water for 15–20 minutes until tender. Drain then sieve or mash.

2 Beat 2 of the eggs. Add butter, cheese, eggs, salt, pepper and nutmeg to the potatoes and mix well together.

3 Shape the potato mixture into 8 croquettes. Beat the remaining egg then dip the croquettes in the egg and roll in breadcrumbs.

4 Heat the oil in a frying pan then fry the croquettes until golden brown on all sides. Serve hot.

• **Fresh herbs can be added to the potato mixture. Chives are particularly good.**

RICOTTA AND NUTMEG DUMPLINGS WITH GORGONZOLA SAUCE

These dumplings are light, fluffy and delicious. Serve with a crisp side salad.

SERVES 6

400 g (14 oz) ricotta cheese
2 tablespoons freshly grated Parmesan cheese
3 egg yolks
1 tablespoon semolina
a good pinch of freshly grated nutmeg
salt and pepper
15 g (½ oz) butter
2 tablespoons double cream
100 g (4 oz) gorgonzola cheese
1 tablespoon chopped fresh parsley

1 In a bowl, mash the ricotta with the Parmesan cheese, egg yolks, semolina, nutmeg, salt and pepper and mix well together.

2 On a lightly oiled surface, roll the paste into thin rolls about 1 cm (½ in) in diameter, then cut with a sharp knife into balls or pieces about 2 cm (¾ in) long.

3 Melt the butter with the cream in a saucepan. Add the gorgonzola cheese and cook over a very low heat, crushing and stirring the cheese until you have a well blended sauce.

4 Lower the dumplings, one at a time, on a slotted spoon into boiling water and let them simmer for about 2 minutes or until they rise to the surface.

5 Serve hot, with the sauce and sprinkled with parsley.

• **Lightly oil your hands before handling the dumplings to prevent them sticking.**

RISOTTO WITH RAISINS AND PINE NUTS

This is a simple, exotic and delicious rice dish, satisfying to cook and eat.

SERVES 4

1 garlic clove

2 shallots

a handful of flat-leaved fresh parsley

1.2 litres (2 pints) vegetable stock (see page 36)

2 tablespoons olive oil

100 ml (4 fl oz) dry white wine

350 g (12 oz) arborio (risotto) rice

75 g (3 oz) raisins

40 g (1½ oz) pine nuts

salt and pepper

25 g (1 oz) butter

75 g (3 oz) freshly grated pecorino cheese
   (optional)

1 Crush the garlic. Finely chop the shallots and parsley. In a large saucepan, bring the stock to the boil and keep just below simmering point.

2 Heat the olive oil in a saucepan and cook the garlic, shallots and parsley over a moderate heat for 5 minutes. Add the white wine and cook over a high heat until it has evaporated.

3 Stir in the rice and add a ladleful of stock and cook until the liquid has been absorbed, stirring constantly. Add another ladleful of stock, the raisins and pine nuts and continue adding the stock, stirring between each addition, until the rice is tender but still firm. This will take about 20 minutes..

4 Season with pepper to taste. Stir in the butter and serve at once with the grated cheese if wished.

• Arborio (risotto) rice is a softer, rounded rice than a basmati rice that's used for Indian dishes. It is supposed to be slightly sticky and produce a creamy dish.

PASTA WITH GARLIC, WALNUT AND ROCKET SAUCE

This is the quickest of sauces – you just whizz the ingredients in the food processor.

SERVES 4

350 g (12 oz) pasta, such as penne or rigatoni

salt

Sauce

250 g (8 oz) walnuts

1 garlic clove

½ teaspoon fresh marjoram leaves

125 ml (4 fl oz) olive oil

125 ml (4 fl oz) double cream

handful of chopped fresh rocket

1 Cook the pasta in plenty of boiling salted water for about 10 minutes until al dente, firm to the bite.

2 Put the walnuts and garlic in a food processor and blend until the nuts are ground. Mix in the marjoram.

3 Put the walnut mixture in a saucepan and stir in the olive oil, cream and rocket. Mix thoroughly then heat gently.

4 Drain the pasta, pour over the hot sauce and serve immediately.

• The walnut and rocket sauce is also delicious served with rice or as a hot dip for steamed vegetables like cauliflower, broccoli and beans.

Clockwise from Top:
Hot broad beans and artichokes with chilli and herbs; Radicchio risotto; Pumpkin fritters with sage and Parmesan; Baked beets with a nut and cheese crumb.

PUMPKIN FRITTERS WITH SAGE AND PARMESAN

Pumpkin has an excellent texture and flavour and is simple to prepare. Yet people buy them for Halloween for lanterns and the glorious orange insides are often thrown away! Here the pumpkin is flavoured and fried.

SERVES 4

750 g (1½ lb) pumpkin flesh

salt and pepper

250 g (8 oz) plain flour

handful of finely chopped fresh sage

100 g (4 oz) freshly grated Parmesan cheese

4 tablespoons olive oil

1 Chop the pumpkin flesh into even cubes, discarding the seeds.

2 Put the flesh in boiling salted water and cook for about 8 minutes until tender. Drain and mash in a bowl. Add the flour, sage, 50g (2oz) of the Parmesan, salt and pepper and knead until smooth.

3 Form into a long sausage and chop into 12 even pieces. Flatten each piece to form a fritter.

4 Heat the oil in a frying pan and fry the fritters for 3–4 minutes on both sides, until golden. Drain well.

5 Serve, sprinkled with the remaining Parmesan cheese.

• **As an alternative to frying, the pumpkin fritters can be boiled in a large saucepan of boiling water for 20 minutes. When they bob up to the top, they are ready.**

BAKED BEETS WITH A NUT AND CHEESE CRUMB

I adore beetroots and think they are so underrated as a vegetable. I think it could be due to the fact that grocers sell them cooked and preserved in vinegar. I advise you to seek out raw beetroots as these are superior.

SERVES 4

6 medium fresh beetroots

75 g (3 oz) mixed nuts

75 g (3 oz) mature cheese (any variety)

3 tablespoons extra virgin olive oil

100 g (4 oz) fresh breadcrumbs

salt and pepper

1 Preheat the oven to 180C (350F/Gas 4). Wash the beetroots very well to remove all soil and grime then bake the beetroots in their skins for 45 minutes.

2 Meanwhile, toast the nuts on a sheet of foil under the grill, turning them frequently. Put in a food processor and blend until finely ground. Grate the cheese. Mix the nuts, cheese, olive oil, breadcrumbs, salt and pepper together in a bowl.

3 Slip the skins off the beetroots and cut into 5 mm (¼ in) thick slices.

4 Now arrange the beetroot slices in a shallow ovenproof dish and top with the breadcrumb mixture.

5 Bake in the oven at 180C (350F/Gas 4) for 20 minutes until golden brown. Serve hot or cold.

• **If you are able to find raw beetroots with their green tops in good condition, the tops are delicious in a salad, or gently steamed.**

HOT BROAD BEANS AND ARTICHOKES WITH CHILLI AND HERBS

I love this combination especially if the artichokes are fresh. However I've given instructions for canned artichokes as you are more likely to be able to buy these.

SERVES 4

450 g (1 lb) broad beans

6 spring onions or ½ a red onion

1 garlic clove

1 very small fresh chilli

6 tablespoons olive oil

handful of chopped fresh parsley

handful of chopped fresh mint

6 cooked artichoke hearts

juice of 1 lemon

a little sugar

salt and pepper

1 Shell the beans. Finely chop the onions and crush the garlic. Chop the chilli, discarding the seeds.

2 Heat the oil in a saucepan and gently fry beans. Add onions, parsley, mint and chilli and fry for 6 minutes.

3 Add artichokes, lemon juice, garlic, sugar, salt and pepper. Add a little water, cover and simmer for 10–15 minutes until the beans are tender. Serve hot, with boiled rice or pasta.

• When buying broad beans, look for small young pods as the beans will then be tender and sweet.

RADICCHIO RISOTTO

Radicchio is so often used just for salads but I like it hot as a vegetable too. I first ate this dish on a warm evening and still remember its scent.

SERVES 4

1 small onion

1 leek

400 g (14 oz) radicchio

1.6 litres (2¾ pints) vegetable stock (see page 36)

3 tablespoons olive oil

100 g (4 oz) butter

400 g (14 oz) arborio (risotto) rice

50 g (2 oz) freshly grated Parmesan cheese

1 teaspoon sugar

salt and pepper

1 Finely chop the onion and leek. Chop the radicchio into small pieces.

2 Bring the stock to the boil and keep just below simmering point.

3 Heat the oil and butter in a medium saucepan. Add the onion and leek and cook until softened. Add the radicchio and stir until coated in butter. Now add the rice and coat in butter, stirring well.

4 Add a ladleful of stock and cook until the liquid has been absorbed. Continue adding the stock, stirring between each addition, until the rice is tender but firm. This will take 20–30 minutes.

5 Add the Parmesan cheese, sugar and season with salt and pepper to taste. Serve immediately.

• A glass of white wine can be used to replace the same quantity of vegetable stock.

RIGATONI WITH GARLIC, ROSEMARY AND MUSHROOMS

This is a rich, creamy Sicilian recipe which is very quick. It always scores ten out of ten with all my family.

SERVES 4

½ an onion

1 small garlic clove

2 sprigs of fresh rosemary

2 celery sticks

175 g (6 oz) flat mushrooms

6 sun dried tomatoes in oil

2 tablespoons olive oil

25 g (1 oz) butter

1 wine glass of dry white wine

salt and pepper

4 tablespoons double cream or creme fraiche

400 g (14 oz) rigatoni or other short cut dried
   pasta

75 g (3 oz) freshly grated Parmesan cheese

1 Finely chop the onion, garlic and 1 sprig of rosemary. Chop the celery and mushrooms. Drain the tomatoes from their oil and finely chop.

2 Heat the olive oil and butter in a large, deep-sided frying pan and fry the onion, garlic and celery for 3 minutes. Now add the mushrooms and fry for 5 minutes. Add the tomatoes, rosemary, wine, salt and pepper. Cover and simmer for 4 minutes.

3 Stir in the cream or creme fraiche and mix well together.

4 Cook the pasta in plenty of boiling water until al dente, firm to the bite. Drain, add to the sauce and mix well.

5 Now add 50 g (2 oz) of the Parmesan cheese and stir well together. Sprinkle with the remaining Parmesan cheese, garnish with the leaves of the remaining rosemary sprig and serve the pasta piping hot.

• Make the sauce in advance and reheat at the last minute.

BROCCOLI AND CAULIFLOWER WITH PARMESAN BATTER

I just adore this method of cooking cauliflower and broccoli – it has to be the all-time best.

SERVES 4

450 g (1 lb) broccoli florets

450 g (1 lb) cauliflower florets

3 large eggs

100 g (4 oz) freshly grated Parmesan cheese

salt and pepper

25 g (1 oz) plain white flour

about 3 tablespoons olive oil, for frying

1 Steam the broccoli 6–8 minutes, until tender. Steam the cauliflower for 6 minutes, until tender. Leave to cool.

2 To make the batter: whisk together the eggs, Parmesan cheese, salt and pepper. When the vegetables are cool, roll in the flour, then dip in the batter.

3 In a frying pan, heat the olive oil and when hot, fry the vegetables until golden and crispy. Drain and serve hot.

• When steaming the vegetables, I add fresh herbs to the water to add flavour.

Top to bottom: *Rigatoni with garlic, rosemary and mushrooms; Penne with pepper and pistachio sauce; Broccoli and cauliflower with Parmesan batter.*

PENNE WITH PEPPER AND PISTACHIO SAUCE

Serve this dish as a starter or part of a main course. I think penne rigate is the best pasta shape for this colourful, tasty sauce.

SERVES 4

3 small yellow and red peppers

4 ripe tomatoes, preferably plum

1 red onion

2 peperoncino

2-3 tablespoons olive oil

2 bay leaves

salt and pepper

400 g (14 oz) dried pasta, such as penne rigate

100 g (4 oz) pistachio nuts

4 tablespoons freshly grated Parmesan cheese

1 Cut the peppers in half, discard the core seeds and cut flesh into bite size chunks.

2 Put the tomatoes in a bowl. Cover with boiling water for about 40 seconds then plunge into cold water. Peel off the skins then chop the flesh. Chop the onion. Crush the peperoncino.

3 Heat the oil in a medium saucepan, add the onion and peppers and fry until softened. Add the peperoncino, tomatoes, bay leaves, salt and pepper. Cover and simmer for 20 minutes.

4 Meanwhile, cook the pasta in plenty of boiling salted water for about 10 minutes until al dente, firm to the bite.

5 Chop the pistachio nuts. When the sauce is cooked, stir in the nuts and adjust the seasoning.

6 Drain the pasta, stir in the sauce and serve with Parmesan cheese.

• **This dish can be made in advance and kept in the fridge for up to 2 days.**

TAGLIATELLE WITH SAFFRON AND MASCARPONE SAUCE

This is a rich creamy dish which is very simple to prepare.

SERVES 6

450-600 g (18-24 oz) tagliatelle

Sauce

2-3 large shallots

1 garlic clove

4 tablespoons olive oil

1 pinch of saffron strands

1 wine glass of dry white wine

450 g (1 lb) mascarpone cheese

salt and pepper

handful of torn fresh basil leaves, to garnish

1 Cook the pasta in plenty of boiling salted water for about 10 minutes until al dente, firm to the bite.

2 Finely chop the shallots and garlic. In a large frying pan heat the oil, add the shallots and garlic and fry for 2-3 minutes.

3 Add the saffron, then half of the wine and finally add the mascarpone cheese. Simmer gently for a few minutes, add the remaining wine, salt and pepper.

4 Drain pasta, add sauce and garnish.

• **The sauce can be kept in the refrigerator for up to 1 week.**

BAKED AUBERGINES WITH HERBY SPINACH AND TOMATO MIDDLES

An excellent starter or maybe main course, simple to prepare, yet totally stunning.

SERVES 4

4 small plump aubergines

2 tablespoons olive oil

350 g (12 oz) fresh tender spinach

large pinch of freshly grated nutmeg

4 tablespoons pesto

25 g (1 oz) pine nuts

salt and pepper

4 medium plum or 2 beefsteak tomatoes

1 red onion

4 frisee leaves

6 large fresh basil leaves

1 Preheat the oven to 180C (350F/Gas 4). Brush aubergines with olive oil and bake for 25 minutes, until cooked.

2 Meanwhile, wash spinach and put in a saucepan. Cook for 5-10 minutes until tender. Drain well then finely chop and put in a bowl. Add nutmeg, pesto, pine nuts, salt and pepper and mix well.

3 Without removing the stalk, slit the aubergines in half lengthways, then cut two more slits on both sides. Fill the outside slits with the spinach and pesto mixture.

4 Slice the tomatoes and slice the onion into rings. Arrange both inside the centre slits of the aubergine, reserving a few tomato slices to garnish. Brush with olive oil.

5 Bake at 190C (375F/Gas 5) for 25 minutes. Arrange on the frisee and reserved tomatoes. Add basil and serve hot.

• **Always wash spinach well in several changes of water to remove any grit and soil. Cook tender summer spinach in only the water that clings to its leaves after rinsing – don't be tempted to add any. Coarser winter spinach needs to have boiling water added.**

LEEK AND TOMATO SOUP WITH CRUSTY BREAD AND BASIL

This is a substantial and filling soup with a delicate flavour.

SERVES 6

6 baby leeks

225 ml (8 fl oz) plus 12 teaspoons olive oil

750 g (1½ lb) fresh ripe tomatoes

salt and pepper

½ teaspoon peperoncino (hot red pepper flakes)

450 g (1 lb) crusty day old bread

750 ml (24 fl oz) vegetable stock (see page 36)

6 fresh basil leaves

1 Slice the leeks and wash well under cold running water.

2 Heat the 50 ml (2 fl oz) oil in a large saucepan, add leeks and fry for 10 minutes.

3 Puree the tomatoes in a blender or food processor and add to the leeks. Add salt and pepper to taste together with the pepper flakes. Simmer for 30 minutes.

4 Cut the bread into small pieces and add it to the pan. Mix well and lightly fry for 5 minutes, then add the stock, mix well and simmer for a further 10 minutes.

5 Serve in individual bowls, add a basil leaf and 2 teaspoons of oil to each serving.

• **When selecting leeks, choose the smaller tender ones as they have more flavour.**

PASTA AND BEAN SOUP

There are many variations of this Classical Italian dish and I think this one is the best.

SERVES 4

6 fresh tomatoes or a 500 ml jar of passata (sieved tomatoes)

1 onion

1 garlic clove

1 chilli

375 g (13 oz) can cannellini beans

4 tablespoons olive oil

200 g (7 oz) dried short pasta (tubetlini is my favourite)

handful of chopped flat-leaved fresh parsley

75 g (3 oz) freshly grated pecorino cheese

1.2 litres (2 pints) vegetable stock (see page 36) or water

salt and pepper

handful of torn fresh basil

1 If using fresh tomatoes, put in a bowl, cover with boiling water for about 30 seconds, then plunge into cold water. Peel off the skins, then chop the flesh, discarding the seeds.

2 Chop the onion. Crush the garlic and chilli. Drain the beans.

3 Heat 2 tablespoons of the olive oil in a large saucepan, add the onions and fry until soft. Add a little salt to draw out the juices. Add the garlic, chilli, tomatoes, beans, pasta, parsley, 50g (2oz) of the cheese, vegetable stock or water, salt and pepper. Bring to the boil and simmer for 20 minutes.

4 Adjust seasoning and stir in remaining olive oil and basil leaves. Serve in soup bowls, sprinkled with the remaining grated pecorino cheese.

• If using dried beans allow 200g (7oz), soak in cold water overnight. The next day, drain, then cook in boiling water for about 1½ hours, until tender. Do not add salt to to the cooking water as it toughens the beans.

AUBERGINE ROLLS WITH GOATS' CHEESE AND TOMATO

Quick and tasty – perfect for a busy life! Serve with steamed seasonal vegetables or a salad and crusty bread.

SERVES 2

1 long aubergine

2 tablespoons olive oil

1 tomato

100 g (4 oz) goats' cheese

handful of finely chopped fresh parsley

salt and pepper

1 Slice the aubergine lengthways. Using 4 inner slices of aubergine, (see tip •) sprinkle the slices with salt and set aside for 20 minutes.

2 Rinse the aubergine slices and pat dry. Brush both sides with olive oil and place on a baking tray. Cook under a preheated grill for 3–4 minutes on each side, until turning brown.

3 Dice the tomato, discarding the seeds. Spread the goats' cheese on the aubergine slices then top with tomato and parsley. Season with pepper. Beginning with a short end roll up the slices. Serve immediately.

• Use the remaining aubergine slices for the Pickled Aubergine recipe on page 136.

Top to bottom: *Pasta and bean soup; Aubergine rolls with goats' cheese and tomato.*

MUSHROOM BURGERS WITH LEEKS AND BLUE CHEESE

This recipe is ideal for a busy person. It is so quick to make and looks impressive.

SERVES 4
900 g (2 lb) flat mushrooms
1 onion
1 garlic clove
handful of fresh parsley
2 tablespoons olive oil
300 ml (½ pint) vegetable stock (see page 36)
about 350 g (12 oz) fresh breadcrumbs
salt and pepper
2 medium leeks
100 g (4 oz) dolcelatte cheese

1 Finely chop the mushrooms, onion, garlic and parsley.

2 In a medium saucepan heat 1 tablespoon of the olive oil, add the onions and lightly fry, until translucent. Now add mushrooms and garlic, stirring well for 3–4 minutes. Now add the stock, cover and simmer for 5 minutes.

3 Put the mushroom mixture in a large mixing bowl, add the breadcrumbs, salt, pepper and parsley and stir well together. The spoon should stand in the mixture – if not, add more breadcrumbs. Cool.

4 Meanwhile, slash leeks lengthways and wash under cold running water. Steam the whole lengths for 3 minutes, until tender.

5 Preheat the oven to 200C (400F/Gas 6). Shape mushroom mixture into 4 burgers. Heat remaining oil in a frying pan, add burgers and fry both sides.

6 Slice the dolcelatte cheese into 4 and place a slice on top of each burger. Wrap in the leeks to form a parcel. Bake for 15 minutes until slightly browned. Serve hot.

• **Make a large batch and freeze or keep in the fridge for up to 3 days.**

ITALIAN GREEN LENTIL SOUP

Serve with bread for a complete meal.

SERVES 6
10 new potatoes, preferably Italian
2 garlic cloves
salt and pepper
225 g (8 oz) green lentils
3 tablespoons olive oil
1 bottle passata or two 397 g cans tomatoes
25 g (1 oz) freshly grated pecorino cheese
4 tablespoons chopped flat-leaved fresh parsley
freshly grated Parmesan cheese, to serve

1 Cut potatoes into even sized cubes, without removing the skins. Crush the garlic.

2 Put the potatoes in a medium saucepan. Add 900 ml (1½ pints) boiling water and season with salt. Cook for 10 minutes.

3 Add the lentils, oil, tomatoes, pepper, garlic and pecorino cheese. Bring to the boil, cover and simmer for 40 minutes.

4 Serve with Parmesan cheese and parsley.

• **Don't be tempted to omit the small quantity of pecorino cheese as it adds a terrific flavour as it melts. Like Parmesan cheese, it can be bought fresh. Wrap it in muslin and store in the fridge – it will keep for weeks.**

CHESTNUT SOUP WITH CHICK PEAS

This is a typical soup of the Molise region of Italy. It is hearty, rich and a complete meal.

SERVES 4
400 g (14 oz) chick peas
450 g (1 lb) fresh chestnuts (see tip •)
3 celery sticks
4 bay leaves
7 tablespoons olive oil
4 garlic cloves
salt and pepper
4 slices of bread

1 Soak the chick peas in water overnight.

2 Preheat the oven to 200C (400F/Gas 6). Score the chestnut skins on the outside and put on a baking tray. Cook in the oven for 40 minutes, then peel off the thick outer skin and thin inner skin.

3 Drain the soaked chick peas then put in a large saucepan with 2.5 litres (4½ pints) water. Add celery, bay leaves and 2 tablespoons oil. Bring to the boil and boil vigorously for 10 minutes.

4 Lower the heat and simmer for 40 minutes, until chick peas are tender and cooking liquid has reduced.

5 Crush the garlic. Heat the remaining oil in a frying pan and fry chestnuts and garlic until golden brown.

6 Remove bay leaves from the soup and stir in the chestnuts, salt and pepper.

7 Toast the bread slices then put in the bottom of a soup tureen and pour over the soup. Leave for 2-3 minutes before serving.

• As an alternative to fresh chestnuts, use canned or dried chestnuts. Canned chestnuts need no preparation but dried chestnuts should be soaked in cold water overnight. The following day, drain, put in a saucepan with fresh water, bring to the boil, cover and simmer for 40 minutes.

SPROUTED BEANS WITH CHINESE LEAF, GINGER AND COCONUT

You can buy sprouted beans or easily grow your own at home. I like mung beans, chick peas and alfalfa sprouts.

SERVES 4
225 g (8 oz) Chinese leaves
1 garlic clove
2 cm (¾ in) piece of fresh ginger
100 g (4 oz) creamed coconut
1 onion
about 1 tablespoon sesame oil
450 g (1 lb) mixed sprouted beans
1 tablespoon shoyu
handful of chopped fresh coriander
cooked rice or rice noodles, to serve

1 Chop the Chinese leaves. Crush the garlic. Peel and grate the ginger. Grate the coconut. Cut the onion in half through the root then slice into half moon segments.

2 Heat a wok or large frying pan, add the oil, cabbage, garlic, ginger, onion, bean sprouts and coriander and stir-fry for 6 minutes.

3 Add the grated coconut and shoyu and stir into the vegetables. Serve at once with rice or rice noodles.

• Beans can be sprouted in a sprouter tray, which I highly recommend, or in a large jar. The sprouts need to be kept cool, dark and well watered. Within a day the beans will sprout. Use quickly while they are crunchy.

Weekend Eating

I like to relax at the weekend and enjoy cooking since I feel under less pressure and usually have more time. These recipes may take a little longer to get ready than something I would cook mid-week but most can be simply served with a crisp fresh salad and some good crusty bread. I've included pizzas, tarts and vegetable bakes – dishes that you can return to for another slice or another helping. Have a good weekend!

ROASTED PEPPERS WITH A PINE NUT AND SULTANA STUFFING

These are truly delicious. Each roasted pepper half is filled with a fruit and nut stuffing and studded with creamy blue cheese. Serve hot or cold with a salad.

SERVES 6

6 large red or yellow peppers

2 tablespoons pine nuts

1 tablespoon capers

2 tablespoons sultanas

small bunch of fresh parsley

4 heaped tablespoons fresh breadcrumbs

225 g (8 oz) dolcelatte cheese

salt and pepper

about 3 tablespoons extra virgin olive oil

1 Preheat the oven to 200C (400F/Gas 6). Put the whole peppers on a baking tray and roast in the oven for about 20 minutes until deflated and slightly charred, turning once during cooking.

2 Meanwhile, toast the pine nuts on a sheet of foil, under the grill, turning them frequently. Chop the capers, sultanas and parsley. Put the cooked peppers in a polythene bag, close and leave them for 10 minutes, then peel off the skins. Cut peppers in half lengthways and remove cores and seeds but keep juice.

3 Put the breadcrumbs in a bowl, add the capers, sultanas, parsley, cheese, pine nuts, salt and pepper and mix together. Add just enough oil and about 4 tablespoons of the reserved juice to bind the mixture.

4 Put a tablespoon of filling on each pepper half and roll up. Arrange the rolls, side by side, on a serving dish and serve cold. Alternatively, to serve hot, put the rolls in a lightly greased ovenproof dish and bake at 190C (375F/Gas 5) for 15–20 minutes.

• These can be made in advance and kept in the fridge for up to 2 days.

PARSLEY AND MOZZARELLA CALZONE

Calzone are folded pizzas and this excellent recipe is from the Bar Mundial in Cassibile, Sicily. Thank you Gianni Fronterre.

SERVES 4

550 g (1¼ lb) strong white unbleached flour

7 g (¼ oz) fresh yeast or 4½ teaspoons dried
   yeast and 1 teaspoon sugar

salt and pepper

100 ml (4 fl oz) olive oil

1 onion

very large handful of flat-leaved fresh parsley

350 g (12 oz) mozzarella cheese

flour, for dusting

1 Cream together the fresh yeast and 175 ml (6 fl oz) hand-hot water. (If using dried yeast, sprinkle it into 175ml (6 fl oz) hand-hot water with the sugar and leave in a warm place for 15 minutes until frothy.)

2 Put the flour and 15 g (½ oz) salt in a large bowl. Add half of the oil and the yeast mixture and mix with a wooden spoon for form a firm dough, adding more water if necessary.

3 Knead for 10 minutes until soft and pliable. Return the dough to a clean bowl.

• Calzone fillings, unlike pizzas, never include tomatoes but they are good served with a tomato pesto (see page 137).

Cover with a clean tea-towel and leave the dough in a warm place to rise for about 1 hour, until it has doubled in size.

4 Meanwhile, prepare the filling. Finely chop the onion. Heat the remaining olive oil in a frying pan, add the onion and fry until soft. Add the parsley and stir for 2 minutes over a medium heat. Season with pepper and set aside. Chop the mozzarella cheese into chunks.

5 Turn the dough on to a lightly floured surface and knead for about 4 minutes to knock out the air bubbles. Roll out into a

rectangle, measuring 38 x 20 cm (15 x 8 in).

6 Add the cheese to the onion then spread the mixture over the dough, leaving a 1 cm (½ in) border around the edges.

7 Now fold the dough lengthways into three and place on a greased baking tray. Leave to rise for 10 minutes.

8 Preheat the oven to 200C (400F/Gas 6). Dust the dough with flour and bake in the oven for 20 minutes, until the calzone is golden brown. Serve hot, warm or cold, cut into squares.

TAGLIATELLE IN A FRESH BASIL AND WALNUT SAUCE

This is a very rich pasta dish. I usually use tagliatelle which are flat, ribbon noodles but for a change I use pappardelle. These are broader noodles which sometimes have wavy edges.

SERVES 4
350 g (12 oz) tagliatelle or pappardelle
salt and pepper
2 sweet ripe tomatoes
2 large garlic cloves
50 g (2 oz) walnut pieces
50 g (2 oz) freshly grated Parmesan cheese plus
   extra, to serve
handful of fresh parsley
4 tablespoons extra virgin olive oil
handful of torn fresh basil leaves
3 tablespoons single cream
sprigs of fresh basil, to garnish

1 Cook the pasta in plenty of boiling salted water as directed on the packet.

2 Put the tomatoes in a bowl, cover with boiling water for about 40 seconds, then plunge into cold water. Peel off the skins. Crush the garlic.

3 Put the tomatoes, garlic, pepper, Parmesan cheese and parsley in a food processor and blend to a smooth paste. Gradually add the olive oil, drop by drop, now add the basil and walnuts.

4 Drain the pasta and toss in the walnut sauce and cream. Garnish with sprigs of basil and serve at once with Parmesan cheese.

• Buy a piece of fresh Parmesan cheese, store it in the fridge and grate it when needed. Cartons of dried Parmesan cheese are a horrid substitute.

CHICKPEA STEW WITH MEDITERRANEAN VEGETABLES AND FENNEL SEEDS

This is a simple but hearty casserole from Italy where it is called Giambotta.

SERVE 4

small aubergine

salt and pepper

½ an onion

2 red peppers

1 garlic clove

1 teaspoon fennel seeds

1 potato

1 courgette

4 tomatoes

3 tablespoons olive oil

227 g (8 oz) can chickpeas

300 ml (½ pint) vegetable stock (see page 36)

1 Cut the aubergine into cubes. Sprinkle with salt, place in a colander, cover and weigh down. Leave for 30 minutes.

2 Meanwhile, chop the onion and peppers, discarding core and seeds. Crush garlic and fennel seeds. Peel and chop potato into cubes. Chop courgette into cubes.

3 Put the tomatoes in a bowl, cover with boiling water for about 30 seconds then plunge into cold water. Peel off the skins, then chop the flesh, discarding the seeds.

4 Rinse the aubergine and pat dry. Heat the oil in a saucepan, add the onion and fry until beginning to brown. Add the garlic and aubergine and fry lightly until the aubergine has changed colour.

5 Now add the peppers, fennel seeds, potatoes, courgettes, tomatoes, chick-peas, stock, salt and pepper. Bring to the boil, cover and simmer for 30 minutes.

• **For extra flavour, replace half the quantity of stock with white wine.**

HOT ASPARAGUS WITH RED PEPPER SAUCE

SERVES 4

2 red peppers

90 ml (3 fl oz) extra virgin olive oil plus extra for sprinkling

a few drops of balsamic vinegar

salt and pepper

750 g (1½ lb) fresh asparagus

a few tarragon leaves, to garnish

1 Preheat the oven to 200C (400F/Gas 6). Put the peppers on a baking tray and roast in the oven for 20–30 minutes, until deflated and slightly charred. Leave to cool then peel off the skins. Cut the peppers in half and discard the core and seeds.

2 Put the peppers and olive oil in a food processor and blend to form a puree. Add vinegar to taste, salt and pepper.

3 Using a potato peeler, shave the length of each asparagus stalk then, if necessary, cut off the end if it is woody.

4 Steam the asparagus for 6–8 minutes, until tender but firm.

5 Arrange asparagus in an ovenproof dish and sprinkle with a little oil. Bake at 190C (375F/Gas 5) for 20 minutes. Pour sauce over asparagus and garnish with tarragon.

• **The sauce can be kept in the fridge for up to 1 week. Balsamic vinegar is a rich, dark vinegar, from Modena in Italy, matured for years like a good wine. It adds an irreplacable something.**

Top to bottom: *Chickpea stew with Mediterranean vegetables and fennel seeds; Hot asparagus with red pepper sauce.*

SPINACH AND CHEESE CRESPOLINI

There are so many versions of this classic dish – this is mine.

SERVES 4
50 g (2 oz) unsalted butter
200 g (7 oz) plain white flour
salt
3 eggs
3 egg yolks
about 300 ml (½ pint) milk
900 g (2 lb) fresh spinach
1 dried chilli or 1 small fresh chilli
1 tablespoon chopped fresh parsley
150 g (5 oz) ricotta cheese
100 g (4 oz) mascarpone cheese
115 g (4½ oz) freshly grated Parmesan cheese
pinch of freshly grated nutmeg

1 To make the pancakes: melt butter. Sift the flour and a pinch of salt into a bowl and make a well in the centre. Beat 2 whole eggs and 2 egg yolks together, then add to the flour with 1 tablespoon of melted butter. Gradually stir in the milk, adding enough to give a smooth batter.

2 In a small frying pan, heat 1 tablespoon of the remaining butter. Pour in just enough batter to cover bottom of pan. Tilt pan so that batter spreads evenly over base. Fry until golden on both sides. Remove from pan and repeat with remaining batter, adding more butter if necessary, to make 8 pancakes.

3 To make the filling: cook the spinach in boiling salted water for 5–10 minutes, until well cooked. Drain well, then chop. Beat remaining whole egg and remaining egg yolk together. Very finely chop chilli.

4 Put the spinach, parsley and ricotta into a bowl and beat well together. Add the mascarpone cheese, 65 g (2½ oz) of the Parmesan cheese, the beaten eggs, chilli, nutmeg and salt and beat well again.

5 Preheat the oven to 200C (400F/Gas 6). Divide the filling between the pancakes, placing it in the centre of each. Fold the edges over the filling to make a parcel.

6 Arrange the pancakes in a buttered ovenproof dish, in a single layer. Sprinkle over the remaining Parmesan cheese. Bake in the oven for 20 minutes, until golden.

• **The pancakes can be made in advance. As you cook them, pile them on top of each other with a sheet of greaseproof in between each one. When cold, wrap in a polythene bag for up to 2 days. Alternatively, the prepared dish can be made in advance, stored in the fridge for up to 1 day then baked. Serve the pancakes piping hot.**

DOLCELATTE AND LEMON DRESSING

The fruitiness of this dressing balances well with the flavour of the cheese.

SERVES 4
50 g (2 oz) dolcelatte cheese
2 tablespoons extra virgin olive oil
grated rind and 2 tablespoons lemon juice
salt and pepper

1 Cut the cheese into cubes and put in a large screw-top jar. Add all the remaining ingredients and shake together. Use as required.

• **Serve this dressing on a crisp Cos lettuce salad or on any of your favourite leaves.**

PARSNIP, LEEK AND CORIANDER SOUP

This is what I call a pure soup – full of natural flavour. I once served it to friends who all, even knowing there was a huge meal ahead, still wanted seconds! It was a very pleasing feeling, especially as it was thrown together.

SERVES 4

2 parsnips

3 medium new potatoes

2 leeks

2 celery sticks

1 medium carrot

2 tablespoons olive oil

large knob of butter

2 tablespoons freshly grated Parmesan cheese

2 tablespoons double cream

1 large handful fresh coriander

chopped fresh parsley, to garnish

1 Chop the parsnips, potatoes, leeks, celery sticks and carrots into even sized chunks.

2 In a large saucepan, heat the olive oil and butter. When hot, add the leeks and cook until wilted.

3 Add the remaining chopped vegetables and cheese and fry until the vegetables have softened slightly, stirring all the time.

4 Add 900 ml (1½ pints) water, bring to the boil then simmer for 40 minutes.

5 Add the cream and fresh coriander and stir well together. Just before serving sprinkle with fresh parsley to garnish.

• This soup may be pureed for an elegant party or served chunky for a rustic soup depending on the occasion.

COLD PEPPERS STUFFED WITH CELERY

This dish looks so impressive as you slice the peppers and arrange them on the plate.

SERVES 4

4 slim, long red peppers

1 celery heart – about 4 sticks

handful of flat-leaved parsley

1 small garlic clove

400 g (14 oz) smooth, full fat soft cheese

salt and pepper

Sauce

handful of mixed fresh herbs, such as fennel, sage, mint, rocket, basil, parsley and dill

4-5 tablespoons extra virgin olive oil

1 Bring a large saucepan of water to the boil, add the whole peppers and boil for 10-12 minutes. Drain and leave to cool.

2 Meanwhile, finely chop the celery, parsley and garlic. Put them in a bowl with the cheese, salt and pepper and mix together until smooth and creamy enough to pipe.

3 When the peppers have cooled, make a 2.5 cm (1 in) slash near the top. Remove the seeds and core then fill a piping bag fitted with a large plain nozzle and pipe the filling mixture into the peppers.

4 To make the sauce, put the mixed herbs and oil in a food processor or blender and process until smooth.

5 To serve, slice the peppers and arrange on individual plates then spoon over a little of the herb sauce.

• If you do not have a food processor, the herbs and oil can be blended by hand in a pestle and mortar.

Clockwise from top:
*White pizza with two
cheeses and basil;
Layered courgette and
barley tortino; Cold
peppers stuffed with
celery; Fried four-
cheese ravioli.*

LAYERED COURGETTE AND BARLEY TORTINO

*This dish tastes so good and looks attractive
with its layers of overlapping courgettes.*

SERVES 4

225 g (8 oz) pearl barley

1 litre (1¾ pints) vegetable stock (see page 36) or
　water

450 g (1 lb) courgettes

2 garlic cloves

3 tablespoons olive oil

50 g (2 oz) butter

6 ripe tomatoes

150 g (5 oz) mozzarella cheese

handful of chopped fresh basil

small handful of chopped fresh mint

150 g (5 oz) freshly grated Parmesan cheese

salt and pepper

50 g (2 oz) fresh white breadcrumbs

1 In a large saucepan, cook the barley in the vegetable stock for 25 minutes, until most of the stock has been absorbed.

2 Thinly slice the courgettes. Crush the garlic. Heat the oil and butter in a frying pan, add the courgettes and garlic and fry until golden. Drain and reserve.

3 Chop the tomatoes and mozzarella cheese and add to the barley with the basil, mint and Parmesan cheese. Season well, with salt and pepper, to taste.

4 Preheat the oven to 200C (400F/Gas 6). To assemble, arrange half the courgettes, in a shallow ovenproof dish, in a neat layer. Now add the barley mixture then a neat layer of the remaining courgettes. Sprinkle over the breadcrumbs. Bake in the oven for 20 minutes, until golden.

• **When layering the barley and courgettes in the dish, you may like to sprinkle over some extra Parmesan cheese.**

FRIED FOUR-CHEESE RAVIOLI

*The recipe for these small fried ravioli – called
Panzarotti – comes from my good friends in
Apulia. Take the time to make your own pasta
dough and enjoy it!*

SERVES 6

450 g (1 lb) plain white or '00' flour

6 large eggs

4 tablespoons extra virgin olive oil

salt and pepper

100 g (4 oz) ricotta cheese

50 g (2 oz) dolcelatte cheese

100 g (4 oz) mozzarella cheese

50 g (2 oz) freshly grated Parmesan cheese

handful of chopped fresh parsley

olive oil, for deep frying

1 To make the pasta dough, put the flour in a bowl, make a well in the centre and break in 4 of the eggs. Add the olive oil and a pinch of salt. Start mixing with a fork, gradually incorporating the flour, then with your hands mix to form a smooth, elastic dough. If it gets too sticky, dust with a little flour. Wrap and leave the dough to rest for 30 minutes.

2 Meanwhile, make the filling. Put the ricotta, dolcelatte, mozzarella and Parmesan cheese, 2 remaining eggs and parsley in a bowl. Season with salt and pepper and mix together.

• **This recipe makes enough for 6 but the ravioli can be made in advance and stored in the fridge for up to 2 days. Fry a batch when needed.**

3 Now roll the dough, on a lightly floured surface, as thinly as you can. Cut into 5cm (2 in) rounds. Place small spoonfuls of the filling 1 cm (½ in) from the edge. Fold into half-moon shapes and, with the prongs of a fork, pinch the edges together. Leave to rest for 30 minutes.

4 Just before serving, heat the oil in a deep-fat fryer and when hot, cook a few at a time for 2-3 minutes until golden brown. Remove from the fryer with a slotted spoon and drain on absorbent kitchen paper. Serve at once.

WHITE PIZZA WITH TWO CHEESES AND BASIL

I like this Pizza. The ingredients are very simple but the taste is so good. It is very popular with all my students.

SERVES 4

40 g (1½ oz) fresh yeast or 4½ teaspoons dried
    yeast and 1 teaspoon sugar
225 g (8 oz) strong white unbleached flour
salt and pepper
100 ml (4 fl oz) olive oil
225 g (8 oz) Gruyere cheese
125 g (4 oz) mozzarella cheese
handful of chopped fresh basil

1 Cream together the fresh yeast and 150 ml (¼ pint) hand-hot water. (If using dried yeast, sprinkle it into 150ml (¼ pint) hand-hot water with the sugar and leave in a warm place for 15 minutes until frothy.)

2 Put the flour on a clean work surface. Mix in 1 teaspoon salt then form into a mound with a hollow in the centre. Pour 75 ml (3 fl oz) of the oil into the hollow followed by the yeast mixture. Mix well, adding more warm water if necessary, to make a soft, springy dough. Knead well for 10 minutes until the dough is smooth.

3 Put the dough in an oiled bowl. Cover with a clean tea-towel and leave to rise in a warm place for about 1 hour, until it has doubled in size.

4 Turn the dough on a lightly floured surface and knead for 5 minutes to knock out the air bubbles. Cut the dough in half. Roll out one half into a 25 cm (10 in) round ten. Repeat with the remaining half.

5 Finely chop the Gruyere and slice the mozzarella cheese. Place half the dough on an oiled baking tray and smother the dough with the cheese and basil. Season with a little salt and pepper. Place the remaining half of the dough on top and seal the edges.

6 Leave the pizza to prove for 10 minutes, until the dough has risen slightly. Preheat the oven to 200C (400F/Gas 6).

7 Drizzle with the remaining olive oil and make fingerprints in the top of the dough to allow the oil to run into the pizza. Bake in the oven for 20-25 minutes, until golden brown. Leave the pizza to cool slightly then serve warm.

• This pizza is also good served cold – ideal for lunchboxes or picnics.

Clockwise from Top:
*Roasted red pepper
Tart; Radicchio and
pecorino pizza; Baked
onions with a parsley
and Parmesan
stuffing.*

BAKED ONIONS WITH A PARSLEY AND PARMESAN STUFFING

This hearty old favourite has a simple stuffing and is delicious served with crusty bread and good butter.

SERVES 4

4 medium onions

100 g (4 oz) freshly grated Parmesan cheese

handful of chopped fresh parsley

2 eggs

75 g (3 oz) butter

salt and pepper

3 tablespoons dry white wine

1 Peel the onions or, if preferred, leave them on to give them a rustic look. Cook in boiling water for 15 minutes, then drain.

2 Preheat the oven to 200C (400F/Gas 6). Cut the onions in half widthways, then scoop out two-thirds of the centres with a spoon. Chop the centres and put in a bowl with the Parmesan cheese, parsley, eggs, 25 g (1 oz) of the butter, salt and pepper. Mix thoroughly, then spoon into the onion shells. Replace the tops.

3 Melt the remaining butter in a flameproof casserole, put the onions in the dish and sprinkle with the wine. Bake in the oven for 30–40 minutes. Serve immediately.

• Choose even-sized onions so that they will be cooked at the same time. They are cooked when just soft, test by prodding with a skewer.

• After roasting, put the peppers in a polythene bag and leave to cool. This will make the peeling of the skins easier.

ROASTED RED PEPPER TART

I deliberately didn't call this a quiche because of the awful image that name conjures up. The peppers are roasted, pureed and blended with cream cheese and chives before being mixed with the eggs. The result is a very lovely pinky red tart.

SERVES 4

200 g (8 oz) plain white unbleached flour

salt and pepper

100 g (4 oz) cold butter

4 large red peppers

1 garlic clove

handful of fresh chives

2 eggs

225 g (8 oz) smooth, full fat, soft cheese

pinch of paprika

1 Preheat the oven to 200C (400F/Gas 6). Sift the flour into a bowl, add a pinch of salt and rub in the butter until the mixture resembles fine breadcrumbs. Gradually add 2–3 tablespoons ice cold water. Do not handle but use a spoon to form the mixture into a ball. Wrap in cling film and chill in the bottom of the fridge for 30 minutes.

2 Meanwhile, put the peppers on a baking tray and roast in the oven for 20 minutes, until deflated and slightly charred, turning once during cooking. Leave to cool.

3 Roll out the pastry and use to line a 20 cm (8 in) loose bottomed flan tin. Prick the base, and line with foil and weigh down with baking beans. Bake in the oven for 15 minutes. Lift out the foil and beans and bake for a further 5 minutes, until firm.

4 Crush the garlic and chop the chives. Now beat the eggs in a bowl and add the garlic, chives, cheese, salt, pepper and paprika and beat together until smooth.

5 Peel the skin off the peppers. Chop the flesh, discarding the core and seeds. Altern-atively, blend the flesh in a food processor, to make a puree.

6 Stir the peppers into the egg and cheese mixture. Pour into the pastry case and bake at 190 C (375F/Gas 5) for 20-25 minutes, until golden.

RADICCHIO AND PECORINO PIZZA

When making Pizza, I go the great lengths to make them as authentic as possible. This is a traditional topping – unusual and colourful!

SERVES 4

40 g (1½ oz) fresh yeast or 4½ teaspoons dried
   yeast and 1 teaspoon sugar
375 g (13 oz) strong white unbleached flour
salt and pepper
4 tablespoons extra virgin olive oil
1 red onion
1.25 kg (2½ lb) radicchio (red chicory)
1 garlic clove
100 g (4 oz) freshly grated pecorino cheese
handful of chopped fresh basil
50 g (2 oz) stoned black olives
100 g (4 oz) mozzarella cheese

1 Cream together the fresh yeast and 150 ml (¼ pint) hand-hot water. (If using dried yeast, sprinkle it into 150ml (¼ pint) hand-hot water with the sugar and leave in a warm place for 15 minutes until frothy.)

2 Put the flour on a clean work surface. Mix in 1 teaspoon salt then form into a mound with a hollow in the centre. Pour the yeast mixture into the hollow, then 2 tablespoons of olive oil. Mix well, adding more water if necessary, to make a stiff but pliable dough. Knead for 10 minutes, until smooth.

3 Put the dough in an oiled bowl. Cover with a clean tea-towel and leave to rise in a warm place for about 1 hour, until it has doubled in size.

4 Finely chop the onion and shred the radicchio. Crush the garlic. In a frying pan, heat 2 tablespoons of the oil. Add the onion and fry until soft. Add the radicchio, garlic and salt and pepper to taste. Cover and cook gently for 15 minutes. Leave it to cool, then add the pecorino cheese and half of the basil.

5 Preheat the oven to 200C (400F/Gas 6). Chop olives and slice mozzarella cheese.

6 When the dough has risen, turn on to a lightly floured surface and knead for 5 minutes to knock out the air bubbles. Roll out into a 25 cm (10 in) round and place on an oiled baking tray. Cover with the radicchio, remaining basil, the olives and then the mozzarella cheese. Leave to rise again for 5 minutes.

7 If you have them, slide the pizza off the tray on to the hot bricks or on to a terracotta baking tray. Bake in the oven for 20-25 minutes, until golden. Leave to cool slightly, before serving.

• Heat some clean oiled bricks in your oven to cook the Pizza on so that you will achieve a crusty base. Some mail order companies sell terracotta baking trays on which to cook Pizza which has the same effect.

Having Friends Round

I love to entertain, in fact, it is one of my greatest pleasures. However, like everyone else, I don't want to spend hours fussing in the kitchen, missing the fun. In this chapter are a collection of recipes that can be prepared in advance or produced at a moments notice. You will be able to spend time with your guests and feed them something that will impress and delight.

Deep fried caper-stuffed olives

These make interesting nibbles or starters but you must buy stoned Queen olives from delicatessen's or larger supermarkets.

SERVES 4

75 g (3 oz) capers

1 small garlic clove

125 g (4 oz) breadcrumbs

handful of finely chopped fresh parsley

salt and pepper

olive oil, for mixing and frying

12 very large stoned green olives

1 large egg

1 tablespoon plain white flour

1 Finely chop the capers. Crush the garlic. Put half the breadcrumbs, the capers, garlic, parsley, salt and pepper in a bowl and mix together. Add a little oil to bind.

2 Using a piping bag fitted with a plain nozzle, stuff the olives with mixture.

3 Now roll the olives in the flour, the egg and then in the remaining breadcrumbs.

4 Heat oil in a frying pan and fry olives until golden brown. Serve hot or cold.

• The olives can be stuffed in advance and served hot or cold.

Glogg

This hot Christmas cordial is a warm red wine drink fortified with Schnapps or vodka.

SERVES 6

1 bottle of red wine

6 tablespoons Schnapps, vodka or other similar
   spirit

piece of fresh root ginger

2 cinnamon sticks

½ teaspoon cardamon seeds

6-8 cloves

6 tablespoons raisins

6 tablespoons blanched almonds

1 Pour the wine and Schnapps or vodka into a saucepan. Peel the ginger and add to the pan with the cinnamon, cardamon and cloves. Leave to marinate for 6 hours or longer.

2 Meanwhile, put the raisins and almonds in small mugs.

3 To serve, heat the mixture until almost boiling. Pour it, piping hot, over the raisins and almonds and serve.

• Hot drinks seem to be much more alcoholic. This mixture is very potent so do be careful!

Mumma

SERVES 6

3 chilled bottles of strong lager

2 chilled bottles of dark beer

6 tablespoons Madeira

1 chilled bottle of sparkling mineral water

1 In a jug, mix together the lager, beer and Madeira.

2 Add the sparkling water and serve at once, in tall glasses.

• For a party, make this drink in batches as you need it.

CREAMY CORN TART WITH CHILLI AND CORIANDER

I think this is perfect for a special occasion and although it takes time to prepare, the result is worth it. The base is a yeast dough flavoured with sage.

SERVES 4

Dough

15 g (½ oz) fresh yeast or 1½ teaspoons dried yeast and a pinch of sugar

40 g (1½ oz) unsalted butter

275 g (10 oz) strong white unbleached flour

salt and pepper

handful of chopped fresh sage

4 eggs

Filling

3 corn on the cobs or 312 g (11 oz) can sweetcorn kernels

225 g (8 oz) mature Cheddar or smoked cheese

1 red onion

1 small chilli

1 tablespoon olive oil

handful of finely chopped fresh coriander

175 ml (6 fl oz) milk

175 ml (6 fl oz) double cream

1 To make the dough, cream together the fresh yeast and 3 tablespoon hand-hot water. (If using dried yeast, sprinkle it into 3 tablespoons hand-hot water with the sugar and leave in a warm place for 15 minutes until frothy).

2 Melt the butter. In a large bowl, mix together the flour and ½ teaspoon salt. Add the sage, 1 of the eggs, melted butter and the yeast liquid and 150ml (¼ pint) hand-hot water. Stir to form a dough.

3 Knead for 10 minutes. Return to a clean bowl, cover with a clean tea-towel and leave to rise in a warm place for about 1 hour until it has doubled in size.

4 If using fresh corn, cut the stalk from the cob and remove the leaves and fine silk. Put the cobs in a saucepan of boiling water and cook for 5-15 minutes, until tender. Using a sharp knife, carefully remove the kernels from the cobs.

5 Now prepare the filling. Grate the cheese. Finely chop the onion. Chop the chilli, discarding the seeds. Heat the oil in a large frying pan, add the onion and cook until softened. Stir in the corn and cook for 5 minutes. Season with salt and pepper.

6 Preheat the oven to 200C (400F/Gas 6). On a lightly floured surface, roll out the dough into a 23 cm (9 in) round. Press it into the bottom of a 28 cm (11 in) loose-bottomed flan tin. Press the dough again, working from the centre of the round and making the sides thicker than the bottom (about 1 cm (½ in) thick). Sprinkle the cheese in the tart with the corn mixture, chilli and coriander.

7 In the bowl, whisk together the remaining 3 eggs, milk, cream and ½ teaspoon salt and pour into the tart.

8 Bake in the oven for 30 minutes, until set and golden brown. Leave to cool slightly before serving warm.

• **To save time, it is a good idea to make the dough in advance and leave it to rise (step 3) overnight in the fridge. Allow the dough to return to room temperature before using it to line the flan tin.**

FRESH PASTA WITH SPINACH, NUTMEG AND PINE NUT FILLING

This dish of fresh pasta, rolled really thinly, spread with filling and rolled up swiss roll style in unusual but delicious. Make it in advance and heat until bubbling under the grill at the last minute.

SERVES 4

Pasta

300 g (11 oz) plain white or '00' flour

3 eggs

Filling

150 g (5 oz) fresh plum tomatoes

1 garlic clove

50 g (2 oz) pine nuts

900 g (2 lb) fresh tender spinach

150 g (5 oz) ricotta cheese

75 g (3 oz) freshly grated pecorino cheese

½ teaspoon freshly grated nutmeg

salt and pepper

50 g (2 oz) unsalted butter

1 To make the pasta: sift the flour and a pinch of salt on to a work surface and make a mound with a hollow in the centre. Beat the eggs together, pour into the hollow and mix to a smooth dough. Knead for 10 minutes then wrap in cling film and leave to rest in the fridge for 30 minutes.

2 Put the tomatoes in a bowl. Cover with boiling water for about 40 seconds then plunge into cold water. Peel off the skins then chop the flesh. Crush the garlic. Toast the pine nuts on a sheet of foil under the grill, turning them frequently. Wash the spinach and put in a saucepan with only the water still clinging to the leaves after washing under cold running water. Cook for 3 minutes then drain.

3 To make the filling, put the tomatoes, garlic, pine nuts, spinach, ricotta cheese, 50 g (2 oz) pecorino cheese, nutmeg, salt and pepper in a bowl and mix together.

4 Flatten the dough with a rolling pin and, on a lightly floured surface, roll out to a rectangle about 3 mm (⅛ in) thick or when you can see the colour of your skin through the pasta.

5 Spread the filling over the dough, leaving a 3 cm (1¼ in) border around the edges. Roll up the dough like a Swiss roll. Wrap in a piece of muslin and secure the ends with thin string.

6 Place the roll in a long narrow, flame-proof casserole and cover with lightly salted cold water. Bring to the boil, lower the heat then simmer for 20 minutes. Remove the casserole from the heat and leave the roll to cool in the water.

7 Remove the muslin and cut the roll into 2 cm (¾ in) slices. Place the slices in a buttered ovenproof dish. Melt the butter. Sprinkle over the remaining pecorino cheese and pour over the butter.

8 Place under a preheated hot grill for 5 minutes. Serve immediately.

• **If you haven't got any muslin use a pale-coloured, clean J cloth to simmer the pasta roll in. Don't use the blue ones – the dye runs!**

Top to bottom: *Chargrilled vegetables layered with cheeses; Fresh pasta with spinach, nutmeg and pine nut stuffing.*

CHAR-GRILLED VEGETABLES LAYERED WITH CHEESES

This is my favourite way of cooking vegetables so that they retain their true flavour. it is quick and simple too.

SERVES 6

2 medium aubergines

salt and pepper

2 medium potatoes

1 medium fennel head

2 red peppers

2 yellow peppers

2 sprigs of rosemary

4 tablespoons extra virgin olive oil

50 g (2 oz) porcini (dried mushrooms)

100 g (4 oz) mozzarella cheese

100 g (4 oz) dolcelatte cheese

grated rind and juice of ½ lemon

300 ml (½ pint) fresh tomato passata

handful of fresh basil

1 garlic clove

crusty bread, to serve

1 Slice the aubergines lengthways. Sprinkle with salt, place in a colander, cover and weigh down. Leave for 30 minutes.

2 Meanwhile, peel and slice the potatoes and steam for 7 minutes. Slice the fennel and steam for 12 minutes.

3 Preheat the oven to 200C (400F/Gas 6). Rinse the aubergines and pat dry. On a large baking tray, arrange the aubergines and potato slices and the red and yellow peppers. Tuck in the rosemary sprigs and pour over 3 tablespoons of the olive oil. Roast the vegetables for 25 minutes, until golden. Leave to cool, then peel the skin off the peppers and slice the flesh, discarding the core and seeds.

4 Meanwhile, soak the porcini in a bowl of warm water for 20 minutes. Thinly slice the mozzarella and dolcelatte cheese. Add the grated lemon rind and juice to the passata. Tear the basil leaves.

5 Drain the porcini. Crush the garlic. Heat the remaining tablespoon of olive oil in a frying pan and lightly fry the porcini. Add the garlic for about 5 minutes, until softened.

6 Using a deep ovenproof dish, assemble the ingredients. Start with a layer of half the aubergine slices, then layers of mozzarella cheese and basil, then spread over the tomato sauce. Add a layer of yellow peppers, the dolcelatte cheese, mushrooms, fennel, potatoes and remaining aubergines. Finish with a layer of the red pepper slices on top.

7 Bake in the oven at 200C (400F/Gas 6) for 20 minutes. Serve hot or warm with crusty bread.

• **This recipe freezes well. Cut into portions when cold, wrap and freeze. Thaw completely then reheat in the oven until piping hot. Tomato passata is a sauce made from tomatoes which have been turned into a puree. It is available from large supermarkets.**

Leek, thyme and pistachio souffles

These light souffles are easy to prepare but look impressive as a main course. Served with hollandaise sauce, the green and yellow colours contrast beautiful.

SERVES 6

400 g (14 oz) young baby leeks

1 tablespoon olive oil

200 ml (7 fl oz) light vegetable stock (see page 36) or water

50 g (2 oz) pistachio nuts

2 large eggs

1 handful of fresh or 2 teaspoons dried thyme

3 tablespoons creme fraiche

salt and pepper

hollandaise Sauce (see below), to serve

sprigs of thyme, to garnish

1 Preheat the oven to 180C (350F/Gas 4). Quarter fill a roasting tin with hot water and place on the middle shelf of the oven. Butter 6 individual 150 ml (¼ pint) ramekin dishes.

2 Finely chop the leeks and wash well. In a large frying pan, heat the olive oil. Add the leeks and cook for 2-3 minutes, until softened. Add the stock or water, cover and cook for a further 5 minutes.

3 Put the pistachio nuts in a food processor and blend until medium ground. Add the leek mixture and puree until smooth. Add the eggs, thyme, creme fraiche, salt and pepper and mix well.

4 Now pour the mixture into the prepared dishes. Place the dishes in the tin of steaming water and bake for 30 minutes.

5 When cooked, loosen the souffles from the sides of the ramekins with a sharp knife. Turn out the souffles on to individual plates and pour a pool of hollandaise sauce on to the plate. Serve, garnished with thyme sprigs.

• **When buying leeks, try to choose small ones as they have more flavour.**

Hollandaise sauce

Serve with savoury souffles (see recipe above) or vegetables such as asparagus, green beans and artichokes.

SERVES 6

100 g (4 oz) unsalted butter

2 teaspoons vinegar

2 teaspoons lemon juice

3 egg yolks

salt and pepper

1 Gently melt the butter. Put the vinegar, lemon juice and egg yolks into a bowl and whisk with a balloon whisk, until well mixed.

2 Place the bowl over a saucepan of hot water and whisk until the mixture is thick and fluffy.

3 Gradually add the butter, whisking after each addition, until the sauce thickens and all the butter has been used. Season with salt and pepper and serve warm.

• **If the sauce shows signs of curdling while you are making it, add a small ice cube and whisk quickly. If it does separate, place a fresh egg yolk in a clean bowl and gradually whisk in the separated sauce, a little at a time.**

POLENTA PIE

Polenta provides warmth and comfort in the winter. On its own it is bland but with the addition of other ingredients, it is quite delicious. This dish takes a bit of time but makes a filling dish.

SERVES 4

salt and pepper

225 g (8 oz) coarse polenta

90 g (3½ oz) butter

2 chopped oregano sprigs

1 small aubergine

1 red pepper

1 courgette

450 g (1 lb) flat mushrooms

3 tablespoons olive oil plus extra for drizzling
   on top

25 g (1 oz) plain white flour

300 ml (10 fl oz) milk

50 g (2 oz) Gruyere cheese

handful of finely chopped flat-leaved fresh
   parsley

100 g (4 oz) freshly grated Parmesan cheese

1 Dampen a 1 kg (2 lb) loaf tin. In a large, heavy saucepan, bring 1.6 litres (2¾ pints) water to simmering point.

2 Add 1½ teaspoons salt to the water then add the polenta, letting it run through your fingers in a thin stream, stirring all the time to prevent lumps forming. Cover and simmer for 30 minutes, stirring vigorously every 5 minutes. The polenta is cooked when it comes away from the sides of the saucepan.

3 Now add 50 g (2 oz) of butter and stir in well. Add salt and pepper and the chopped oregano. Stir until the butter has melted.

Pour into the loaf tin and leave to set for 20–30 minutes.

4 Preheat the oven to 200C (400F/Gas 6). Slice the aubergine lengthways. Sprinkle with salt, place in a colander, cover and weigh down. Leave for 30 minutes.

5 Meanwhile, put the red pepper on a baking tray and roast in the oven for 20 minutes until slightly blackened and deflated, turning once during cooking. Leave to cool.

6 Slice the courgette lengthways and slice the mushrooms. Heat the oil in a frying pan and fry the courgette slices, then drain and reserve. Now fry the mushrooms until tender, season with salt and pepper and reserve. Rinse the aubergine slices, pat dry and fry until golden. Drain and reserve. When pepper is cool, peel off skin and chop flesh, discarding core and seeds.

7 Now make the sauce. Grate the Gruyere cheese. In a saucepan, melt the remaining 40g (1½ oz) of butter, add the flour and cook the roux for 3 minutes, stirring. Remove the pan from the heat and gradually beat in milk. Return to the heat and slowly bring to the boil, beating all the time, until thickened. Stir in cheese, mushrooms, salt and pepper.

8 Turn the set polenta out of the tin on to a board and cut into 5 slices lengthways. Layer the polenta, filling and sauce with Parmesan cheese in the loaf tin. Drizzle on some olive oil and bake in the oven at 200C (400F/Gas 6) for 20 minutes.

• **Polenta is made from cornmeal or maize flour and fine, medium and coarse varieties are available. Instant polenta which cooks in 5 minutes, is also available but is no substitute for the real thing. To save time, prepare the polenta the day before it is needed.**

Top to bottom:
Polenta pie; Artichoke tart with Gruyere.

ARTICHOKE TART WITH GRUYERE

I love tarts and pies. I think they can look impressive and yet they are so easy to make.

SERVES 4
4 eggs and 1 egg yolk
1 teaspoon sugar
250 g (9 oz) plain white unbleached flour
1 teaspoon salt
65 g (2½ oz) unsalted butter
1 small onion
2 tablespoons olive oil
8 fresh or canned artichoke hearts
200 g (7 oz) Gruyere cheese
handful of fresh flat-leaved parsley
salt and pepper

1 To make the pastry, put the egg yolk, sugar and 65 ml (2½ fl oz) cold water in a bowl and mix together.

2 Sift the flour and salt into a separate bowl and rub in the butter until the mixture resembles fine breadcrumbs.

3 Make a hollow in the centre and add the egg yolk mixture. Mix with a spoon until the mixture holds together, adding more water, if necessary. Knead very lightly.

4 To make the tart, roll out the pastry on a lightly floured surface and use to line a 20 – 22 cm (8 – 8½ in) flan dish or tin. Prick the base with a fork and place in the fridge to rest for 30 minutes.

5 Meanwhile, slice the onion. In a frying pan, heat the oil, add onion and fry for 5 minutes. Add artichokes and cook gently for 10 minutes. Leave to cool.

6 Preheat the oven to 200C (400F/Gas 6). Line the pastry base with foil and weigh down with baking beans. Bake in the oven for about 10 minutes, until set.

7 Meanwhile, grate the cheese and finely chop parsley. Now beat the 4 eggs in a bowl, add the cheese, parsley, salt and pepper and beat together. Add the artichoke mixture. Pour into the pastry case and cook for 25 minutes, until golden.

• If wished, you can make individual tarts by linings and filling 4 individual tins. Reduce the cooking time to 15-20 minutes.

CELEBRATION PIZZAS

MAKES 6
500 g (1 lb) fresh or frozen puff pastry, thawed if frozen
⅓ quantity of tomato sauce from Lasagne recipe (see page 98)
12 fresh basil leaves
12 thin slices of mozzarella cheese
pepper

1 Preheat oven to 200C (400F/Gas 6). Roll out the puff pastry into six 10 cm (4 in) circles.

2 Spread a little tomato sauce over the pastry, top with some basil leaves and slices of mozzarella. Sprinkle with pepper. Bake for 12 minutes, until golden.

• These Pizzas can have various toppings added to them such as fried mushrooms or roasted peppers.

POTATO AND MUSHROOM LAYER CAKE

This recipe is a favourite with everyone who's eaten it or tested it for me. I layer garlicky mushrooms, roasted peppers, waxy potatoes and mozzarella in a cake tin and bake it in the oven. The result is a meal in itself.

SERVES 6

1 onion

2 garlic cloves

225 g (8 oz) flat mushrooms

2 tablespoons olive oil

salt and pepper

2 tablespoons finely chopped fresh parsley

handful of chopped fresh basil

1 red pepper

1 yellow pepper

900 g (2 lb) new potatoes

175 g (6 oz) mozzarella cheese

25 g (1 oz) fresh breadcrumbs

50 g (2 oz) freshly grated Parmesan cheese

1 Preheat the oven to 200C (400F/Gas 6). Grease a 15 cm (6 in) round loose-bottomed or spring release tin.

2 Finely chop the onion. Crush the garlic. Slice the mushrooms. In a large frying pan, heat 1 tablespoon of the oil and cook the onion. When cooked, add the garlic and mushrooms. Season well with salt and pepper, add the parsley and basil and set aside.

3 Put the whole red and yellow pepper on a baking tray and bake in the oven for 20 minutes, until slightly blackened and deflated, turning once during cooking. Leave to cool.

4 Scrub the potatoes then cook in boiling water until tender. Leave to cool.

5 When the peppers are cool, peel off the skins and slice the flesh, discarding the core and seeds. Slice the potatoes and cheese.

6 Cover the base of the tin with half the breadcrumbs, then half the potato slices, half the onion mixture, half the peppers and half the mozzarella cheese. Repeat the layers and keep pressing down to keep all the ingredients tightly in the tin.

7 Finally, sprinkle over the remaining oil and the breadcrumbs and Parmesan cheese. Give a final press and bake in the oven at 190C (375F/Gas 5) for 20–25 minutes until golden. Serve hot.

• If making in advance, make to the end of step 6, cover and weight down with a can or measuring scale weights. Bake when needed.

Clockwise from top:
*Potato mountain pie
with rosemary; Fat
Freddies pumpkin;
Green sauce with
capers and herbs.*

POTATO MOUNTAIN PIE WITH ROSEMARY

This pie is very eye-catching especially if you garnish it with salad ingredients like parsley, frisee, rocket and cherry tomatoes.

SERVES 4-6

175 g (6 oz) wholemeal or white flour

salt and pepper

100 g (4 oz) butter

pinch of sugar

2 tablespoons olive oil

1 medium red pepper

1.2 kg (2½ lb) new potatoes

450 g (1 lb) leeks

1 garlic clove

50 g (2 oz) ground almonds

225 g (8 oz) flat mushrooms

handful of fresh rosemary

175 g (6 oz) mature Cheddar cheese

handful of flat-leaved fresh parsley

pinch of paprika

2 large eggs

1 Preheat the oven to 200C (400F/Gas 6). To make the pastry: mix the flour and salt in a large bowl. Rub in 75 g (3 oz) of the butter until the mixture resembles fine breadcrumbs.

2 In another bowl mix 2 tablespoons iced water with the sugar and 1 tablespoon of the oil. Make a reservoir in the flour mixture, pour in the water mixture and, using a spoon, combine gently. Form into a soft damp ball.

3 Wrap the pastry in greaseproof paper and chill for 30 minutes.

4 To prepare filling, put pepper on a baking tray and roast in oven for about 25 minutes,

turning once during cooking. Leave to cool for about 25 minutes then peel off skin and chop flesh.

5 Scrub the potatoes then cut into evenly sized pieces and steam for 5–10 minutes, until tender.

6 Finely shred leeks. Crush the garlic. Heat remaining oil in a large frying pan, add leeks and lightly fry for 5 minutes, until soft, then add crushed garlic and ground almonds.

7 Heat the remaining butter in a saucepan, add mushrooms with plenty of salt and pepper and a little of the rosemary and lightly fry for 5 minutes.

8 Roll out the pastry and use to line an 18 cm (7 in) flan dish. Prick base with a fork then bake blind in the oven at 200C (400F/Gas 6) for 10 minutes.

9 Grate the cheese. To assemble: cover the base with one-third of the potato. Add a layer of leeks, a quarter of the cheese, the remaining rosemary and red pepper. Then add another one-third of the potato, a quarter of the cheese, the parsley, mushrooms, a quarter of the cheese, remaining potato and then the remaining cheese. (Press the potato layers gently to flatten them). The finished mountain should be roughly conical in shape. Sprinkle with paprika, beat the egg and pour over the top.

10 Bake at 200C (400F/Gas 6) for about 25 minutes, until golden brown.

• A variety of new potatoes can be used in this recipe. Look out for Jersey Royals which appear in the shops in May and Pentland Javelin which are available a month later. To save time, the complete pie can be made in advance but don't pour over the egg until just before serving.

FAT FREDDIES PUMPKIN

This recipe was given to me by a New Zealand friend – Kaylee – a fellow pumpkin lover. You stuff and bake the pumpkin and take it to the table whole. It looks impressive! Cut it into wedges – like a melon – to serve.

SERVES 4

1 whole pumpkin, weighing 1-2 kg (2-4 lb)

3-4 thin slices of wholemeal bread

1 tablespoon olive oil

25 g (1 oz) butter

1½-2 teaspoons Marmite or Miso

1 egg

285 ml (10fl oz) carton fresh soured cream

1 teaspoon freshly grated nutmeg

two teaspoons (1 of each) of your favourite dried
 herbs, such as thyme and mint

handful of chopped fresh flat-leaved parsley

salt and pepper

50 g (2 oz) Gruyere cheese

50 g (2 oz) Cheddar cheese

1 Preheat the oven to 200C (400F/Gas 6). Cut top off the pumpkin to make a lid. Scoop out the seeds and discard.

2 Cut the bread into cubes, the size of croutons. Heat the oil and butter in a frying pan, add the bread cubes and lightly fry until brown. Pile into the pumpkin cavity.

3 Dissolve Marmite or Miso in 300 ml (½ pint) hot water and pour into pumpkin. (It should three-quarters fill the cavity).

4 In a bowl, beat together the egg, soured cream, nutmeg, herbs, parsley, salt, pepper and cheeses. Add to the pumpkin cavity and stir gently.

5 Replace lid and put pumpkin in a roasting tin. Cook for 1½ hours, until tender. To serve, remove the lid and cut into wedges.

• If you can, find a pumpkin with a stalk as this makes it easier to lift the lid when serving.

GREEN SAUCE WITH CAPERS AND HERBS

This can be served as a dip for a starter with crusty bread or crudites or with pasta.

SERVES 4

4 pickled cucumbers

1 large bunch of flat-leaved parsley

25 g (1 oz) fresh mint

25 g (1 oz) capers

2 eggs, hard-boiled

4 tablespoons fresh breadcrumbs

2 garlic cloves

2 tablespoons white wine vinegar

1 tablespoon sugar

8 tablespoons extra virgin olive oil

salt and pepper

1 Finely chop the cucumbers, parsley, mint and capers. Mash the hard-boiled eggs.

2 Put all the ingredients in a food processor and blend everything together to produce a smooth, green sauce. Serve hot or cold.

• The sauce can be kept in the fridge for up to 2 weeks but make sure the ingredients are always covered with oil to preserve them.

A CAKE OF AUBERGINE AND COURGETTES

One of my all time favourites – aubergine and courgette slices, fried in an egg and Parmesan coating until golden and crispy, then layered with a fresh tomato sauce and mozzarella cheese. Just bake until bubbling and serve hot with a crisp green salad and crusty bread.

SERVES 4

1 medium aubergine

2 courgettes

salt and pepper

900 g (2 lb) fresh ripe tomatoes

1 onion

1 garlic clove

6 tablespoons olive oil

1 teaspoon sugar

1 handful of torn fresh basil leaves

2 tablespoons plain white unbleached flour

4 eggs

3 tablespoons freshly grated Parmesan cheese,
    plus extra to sprinkle on top

two 175 g (6 oz) packets mozzarella cheese

1 Thinly slice the aubergine and slice the courgettes lengthways. Sprinkle with salt, place in a colander, cover and weigh down. Leave for 30 minutes.

2 Put the tomatoes in a bowl, cover with boiling water for about 40 seconds, then plunge into cold water. Using a sharp knife, peel off the skins.

3 Finely chop the onion. Crush the garlic. In a large saucepan, heat 2 tablespoons of olive oil, add the garlic and cook until coloured, then add the onion and cook gently until softened. Add the tomatoes and sugar, bring to the boil, then simmer for 40 minutes, uncovered to allow the sauce to reduce. Season with salt and pepper and add a few basil leaves. The sauce should be thick and concentrated.

4 Rinse the aubergine and courgettes and pat dry. Dip the vegetables in flour and set aside.

5 Whisk the eggs in a bowl and add the Parmesan cheese. In a frying pan, heat the oil. Dip the aubergine and courgettes in the egg mixture and fry until golden on both sides. Drain on absorbent kitchen paper and set aside.

6 Preheat the oven to 190C (375F/Gas 5). Slice the mozzarella cheese.

7 Assemble the dish by layering the ingredients in a 20 cm (8 in) spring release cake tin. Place a third of the aubergines in the bottom, add half the courgettes and a third of the cheese, tomato sauce and basil leaves. Then add a layer of aubergines, cheese, tomato sauce, basil leaves, remaining courgettes, cheese, tomato sauce, basil leaves and finally aubergines.

8 Sprinkle over Parmesan cheese and bake in the oven for 20–25 minutes until golden.

• Make this in advance and reheat at the last minute. It's the sort of dish that doesn't spoil if guests are late. Mozzarella is an unripened cheese made from cows' milk although genuine mozzarella is made from buffaloes' milk. It is made all over Italy and traditionally shaped into balls, which are kept in whey and sold from the bowl. Mozzarella made in other countries are a poor substitute as they are often rubbery and do not have the same melting qualities.

Top to bottom: *A cake of aubergine and courgettes; Shallot, spinach and mushroom tian.*

SHALLOT, SPINACH AND MUSHROOM TIAN

I love this savoury bake which is finished in the oven with eggs and topped with cheese and breadcrumbs.

SERVES 6

450 g (1 lb) fresh tender spinach

6 shallots

225 g (8 oz) browncap mushrooms

3 courgettes

1 garlic clove

3 tablespoons olive oil

1.1 litres (2 pints) vegetable stock (see page 36) or water

225 g (8 oz) arborio (risotto) rice

3 eggs

125 g (4 oz) mature cheese, such as Gruyere or Cheddar

pinch of freshly grated nutmeg

salt and pepper

3 tablespoons fresh breadcrumbs

1 Wash the spinach and put in a saucepan with only the water still clinging to the leaves after washing under cold running water. Cook for 5 minutes, then drain.

2 Finely slice the shallots. Roughly chop the mushrooms and finely chop the courgettes. Crush the garlic. Heat oil in a saucepan, add shallots, mushrooms and courgettes and cook gently for 5 minutes. Add garlic and spinach and cook for a further 5 minutes.

3 Meanwhile, bring the stock to the boil and keep just below simmering point.

4 Stir the rice into the vegetables, then add a ladleful of stock and cook until the liquid has been absorbed. Continue adding the stock, stirring between each addition, until the rice is tender but firm. This will take about 30 minutes. Remove from the heat.

5 Preheat the oven to 200C (400F/Gas 6). Beat the eggs. Grate the cheese and add to the spinach, reserving a little. Add the eggs, nutmeg, salt and pepper and mix together.

6 Spoon the mixture into a greased ovenproof dish. Sprinkle with breadcrumbs and reserved cheese. Bake for 30 minutes.

• A Tian is a traditional Provencal dish which takes its name from the earthenware gratin dish in which it is cooked.

A CAKE OF PASTA AND SPINACH

SERVES 4

450 g (1 lb) plain white or '00' Italian flour

salt and pepper

5 eggs plus 1 egg yolk, for glazing

1 teaspoon extra virgin olive oil

4 teaspoons warm milk

450 g (1 lb) fresh tender spinach or chard (see tip •)

50 g (2 oz) freshly grated Parmesan cheese

100 g (4 oz) ricotta cheese

pinch of freshly grated nutmeg

1 To make the pasta, put the flour and 1 teaspoon of salt on to a work surface and make a mound with a hollow in the centre. Beat 3 of the eggs together and pour into the hollow. Add the olive oil, warm milk and a little water and mix to a smooth dough, adding more water if necessary. Knead for 10 minutes then wrap in cling film and leave in fridge for 30 minutes.

2 To make the filling, wash the spinach and

• Swiss chard can be used as an alternative to spinach. Cut out the triangular white core and use for stir fries, use the leaves as you would spinach.

put in a saucepan with only the water still clinging to the leaves after washing. Cook for 5 minutes then drain well, squeezing out the excess water.

3 Finely chop the spinach and put in a bowl. Add the remaining 2 eggs, Parmesan and ricotta cheese, nutmeg, salt and pepper and mix well together.

4 Divide dough in two and cover one half. Flatten remaining dough with a rolling pin and, on a lightly floured surface, roll out to a rectangle until you can see the colour of the skin of your hand beneath it.

5 Lay the dough in a shallow baking tray then roll out the remaining dough, for the lid, in the same way.

6 Preheat the oven to 200C (400F/Gas 6). Spread the spinach filling evenly over the dough. Lay the second piece of dough over the top and pinch the sides together, to seal. Make 3 slashes in the top of the dough and brush with beaten egg yolk. Bake in the oven for 20-25 minutes, until golden brown. Serve hot.

GRANDMOTHER FURIANI'S RADICCHIO LASAGNE

I spent a fantastic weekend in Verona, staying with a family who produce the best radicchio I have ever seen and tasted. The Grandmother of the family taught me how to cook and use radicchio in a way that I had never considered.

SERVES 4

1 onion

2 radicchio (red chicory)

olive oil, for frying

salt and pepper

10 sheets of fresh, dried or oven-ready lasagne

Sauce

40 g (1½ oz) butter

25 g (1 oz) plain white flour

300 ml (10 fl oz) milk

225 g (8 oz) freshly grated Parmesan or Gruyere cheese

1 teaspoon freshly grated nutmeg

1 Chop the onion. Finely slice the radicchio. Heat a little oil in a frying pan, add the onion and fry until golden. Add the radicchio and fry for 4-6 minutes, until the radicchio has wilted. Add salt and pepper.

2 Cook the lasagne as directed on the packet, then drain well.

3 To make the white sauce, melt the butter in a saucepan, add the flour and cook for 2-3 minutes, stirring. Remove the pan from the heat and gradually beat in the milk. Return to the heat and slowly bring to the boil, stirring all the time, until the sauce boils and thickens. Stir in three-quarters of the cheese, radicchio mixture and nutmeg.

4 Preheat the oven to 190C (375F/Gas 5). Put a layer of sauce in the bottom of a square ovenproof dish. Place a layer of lasagne on top and then add a layer of radicchio mixture. Continue making layers, finishing with sauce. Cover top with remaining cheese. Bake for 25 minutes, until golden.

• For a special occasion, use half milk and half cream to make the sauce.

MUSHROOM LASAGNE WITH ROASTED PEPPERS AND RICOTTA

This is a lasagne with a difference. Like all lasagnes it is fiddly to make but it's ideal for entertaining because it can be made in advance and doesn't spoil if it's kept waiting.

SERVES 4

225 g (8 oz) fresh mushroom or 75 g (3 oz) dried
   wild mushrooms

1 aubergine, weighing about 250 g (9 oz)

salt and pepper

2 red peppers

5-6 tablespoons olive oil

10 sheets of fresh or dried lasagne

salt and pepper

900 g (2 lb) ripe fresh tomatoes

1 red onion

1 garlic clove

about 225 g (8 oz) mozzarella cheese

2 tablespoons dry white wine

1 tablespoon tomato paste

handful of torn fresh basil

450 g (1 lb) ricotta cheese

75 g (3 oz) freshly grated Parmesan cheese

1 Preheat the oven to 200C (400F/Gas 6). Slice fresh mushrooms. If using dried mushrooms, reconstitute in warm water and pat dry.

2 Slice the aubergine lengthways. Sprinkle with salt, place in a colander, cover and weigh down. Leave for 30 minutes.

3 Put the peppers on a baking tray and roast in the oven for 20–25 minutes, until deflated and slightly charred. Leave to cool then peel off the skins. Cut the peppers in half, discarding the core and seeds then thinly slice the flesh.

4 Heat about 1 tablespoon of olive oil in a frying pan, add the fresh or dried mushrooms and fry until softened. Cook the lasagne sheets in boiling salted water for 3–4 minutes. Drain well.

5 Put the tomatoes in a bowl. Cover with boiling water for about 40 seconds then plunge into cold water. Peel off the skins then chop the flesh. Chop the onion and crush the garlic. Slice the mozzarella cheese.

6 To make the tomato sauce, heat 2 tablespoons of oil in a saucepan. Add the tomatoes, onion and garlic, cover and cook gently, stirring, for 10 minutes. Add 300 ml (½ pint) water, the wine, tomato paste, salt and pepper. Half cover and simmer for 30 minutes. If wished, sieve sauce.

7 Rinse the aubergine slices well and pat dry. Heat the remaining oil in a frying pan and fry the aubergine slices on both sides, until golden. Drain on kitchen paper.

8 Preheat the oven to 190C (375F/Gas 5). To assemble the dish, put one-third of the sauce in the bottom of a shallow ovenproof dish. Sprinkle on half the basil leaves. Now add half the aubergine slices, pepper slices, lasagne sheets, ricotta cheese and half of the mushrooms. Repeat these layers, finishing with a layer of tomato sauce. Cover the dish with the slices of mozzarella cheese and sprinkle with Parmesan cheese.

9 Bake in the oven for 25 minutes, until golden and bubbling.

• Sprinkling the aubergines with salt draws out their moisture and removes any bitter flavour. This is not always neccessary as aubergines tend not to be bitter these days – especially smaller ones. If you are short of time you can skip this stage.

Mushroom lasagne with roasted peppers and ricotta.

APPLE, ALMOND AND SOURED CREAM CAKE

This cake appears rather special yet you will be surprised how quick it is to make.

SERVES 4 – 6

1 tablespoon demerara sugar

2 large eggs

125 g (4 oz) butter

125 g (4 oz) caster sugar

2 drops of natural vanilla essence

125 g (4 oz) ground almonds

50 g (2 oz) self raising flour

150 ml (¼ pint) soured cream

175 g (6 oz) Cox's orange pippin or Braeburn
   apples

whipped cream, to serve

1 Preheat the oven to 180C (350F/Gas 4). Grease and line a 20 cm (8 in) deep sandwich tin with baking parchment then sprinkle with the demerara sugar.

2 Separate the eggs. Cream together the butter and sugar until light and fluffy. Beat in the egg yolks and vanilla essence then fold in the almonds, flour and soured cream.

3 Whisk the egg whites until they hold their shape then, using a metal spoon, fold into the creamed mixture.

4 Peel, core and slice the apples and arrange in the base of the prepared tin.

5 Spoon the creamed mixture over the apples and level the surface. Bake for 45 minutes-1 hour until golden and firm to touch.

6 Invert on to a warmed serving plate and serve warm with whipped cream.

• You can make your own soured cream by adding 1 teaspoon lemon juice to 150 ml (¼ pint) single cream. Leave to stand for 30 minutes.

WICKED COFFEE FUDGE PUDDING

This pudding separates during cooking to produce a fudge sauce topped with sponge.

SERVES 6 – 8

225 g (8 oz) butter

350 g (12 oz) soft brown sugar

2 large eggs

6 tablespoons strong black coffee

1 tablespoon cocoa powder

225 g (8 oz) self raising flour

300 ml (½ pint) milk

1 Preheat the oven to 170C (325F/Gas 3). Lightly grease a 1.2 litre (2 pint) ovenproof dish.

2 Put butter and 225 g (8 oz) of the sugar in a bowl and cream together until light and fluffy. Beat the eggs and add to the mixture, a little at a time. Beat in the coffee. Sift together the cocoa powder and flour then fold into mixture, a little at a time. Add 2-3 tablespoons of the milk to give a soft dropping consistency.

3 Spoon the mixture into the prepared dish. Mix together the remaining sugar and milk and pour evenly over the pudding mixture.

4 Bake for 1 hour until top is set and spongy to the touch. Serve warm.

• This is the most wonderful family meal pudding but for a formal occasion, cook it in individual ramekin dishes.

HONEY ICE CREAM

Custard-based ice creams are my favourite. This one is rich and smooth – a real treat!

SERVES 6

3 large eggs

3 tablespoons honey

300 ml (½ pint) milk

300 ml (½ pint) double or whipping cream

1 Beat the eggs and honey together. Heat the milk in a saucepan until just before boiling then pour it on to the egg mixture, stirring constantly.

2 Strain the mixture back into the pan and cook over a gentle heat, stirring, until the custard is smooth and coats the back of a wooden spoon. Cover with a piece of greaseproof paper and leave to cool.

3 When cold, whip the cream until stiff then fold into the custard. Pour into a freezer container and freeze for 3 hours until frozen. Alternatively, pour the mixture into an ice cream machine and freeze according to the manufacturer's instructions.

• For an added treat, serve with chocolate sauce. It is also very good served with sliced fresh peaches when in season.

BOOZY STUFFED PRUNES DRIZZLED WITH CHOCOLATE

Prunes are so often neglected so I am continuing my quest for them to be taken more seriously as a delicious fruit. Pruneaux D'Agen from France are my favourites. Serve these with coffee or ice cream as a dessert.

SERVES 6

18 prunes, preferably unsulphured

300 ml (½ pint) dessert wine

50 g (2 oz) blanched almonds

grated rind of 2 oranges

100 g (4 oz) mascarpone cheese

50 g (2 oz) plain chocolate

50 g (2 oz) white chocolate

icing sugar, to dust

1 Put the prunes in a bowl, pour over the wine and leave to soak overnight.

2 Toast the almonds on a sheet of foil under the grill, turning them frequently. Leave to cool then finely chop.

3 The next day, drain the prunes and dry with kitchen paper, then remove the stones. Put in a bowl, add the orange rind, cheese and almonds and mix together. Use the mixture to fill the prunes.

4 Break the plain chocolate into a bowl, place over a saucepan of hot water, stirring occasionally until smooth. Melt the white chocolate in the same way.

5 Roll the prunes in the plain chocolate and place on baking parchment to dry.

6 Fill a piping bag, fitted with a small plain nozzle, with white chocolate and pipe lines on the prunes. Alternatively, using a teaspoon, drizzle the white chocolate over the prunes. Leave to dry.

7 To serve, arrange 3 prunes on a plate and dust with a little icing sugar.

• Don't waste the wine used for soaking the prunes. Squeeze the juice from the oranges from which the rind has been removed, add to the wine and chill well before drinking.

Clockwise from top:
*Baked chocolate
cheesecake with
vanilla and pecan
nuts; Chocolate and
chestnut torte;
Chocolate polenta
cake.*

CHOCOLATE POLENTA CAKE

This is quite the best chocolate cake I know!

SERVES 6
flour, for dusting
400 g (14 oz) plain chocolate
175 g (7 oz) unsalted butter
5 eggs, size 3
150 g (5 oz) caster sugar
60 ml (2 fl oz) rum or brandy
100 g (4 oz) fine polenta
chocolate caraque, to decorate

1 Preheat the oven to 180C (350F/Gas 4). Grease 25 cm (10 in) loose bottomed cake tin. Dust with flour.

2 Break 225 g (8 oz) chocolate into a bowl and add 100 g (4 oz) butter. Place over a saucepan of simmering water until smooth, stirring.

3 Separate the eggs. Add sugar to yolks and whisk until pale. Fold into chocolate mixture and add rum. Whisk egg whites until stiff then fold into chocolate mixture. Fold in polenta and pour into tin.

4 Bake in the oven for 40 minutes. Leave to cool (it will sink in the centre).

5 To make the glaze, break remaining chocolate in a bowl and add remaining butter. Melt as before then pour over cake and smooth top and sides with a palette knife. Leave to set but do not refrigerate. When set, arrange caraque on top.

• Polenta is a yellow grain made from cornmeal or maize flour. Coarse, medium and fine varieties are available. Buy fine polenta for this cake. It gives it such a good texture and great keeping qualities. The cake will keep for up to 1 month in a tin.

BAKED CHOCOLATE CHEESECAKE WITH VANILLA AND PECAN NUTS

For all chocolate – and cheescake lovers – in moderation, of course! This pudding has a dense, fudgy texture.

SERVES 6
100 g (4 oz) Digestive biscuits
250 g (9 oz) plain chocolate
200 g (7 oz) unsalted butter
150 ml (5 fl oz) soured cream
½ teaspoon vanilla essence
125 g (4 oz) pecan nuts
2 large eggs
125 g (4 oz) caster sugar
500 g (1 lb) cream cheese
whipping cream and pecan nuts, to decorate

1 To make the crust, put the biscuits in a strong polythene bag and crush with a rolling pin. Grate 25 g (1 oz) of the chocolate. Melt 75 g (3 oz) of butter, add the crumbs and chocolate and mix the ingredients well together.

2 Press the mixture into the bottom of a 23 cm (9 in) spring release cake tin.

3 To make the filling, break the remaining chocolate into a bowl and add the remaining butter. Place over a saucepan of simmering water until the mixture is smooth, stirring all the time. Stir in the soured cream and vanilla and heat gently then remove from the heat.

• Buy the darkest, best quality chocolate you can afford. The higher the fat content, the better the chocolate, so look for something that's at least 50% cocoa butter.

4 Preheat the oven to 170C (325F/Gas 3). Chop the nuts.

5 Put the eggs and sugar in a bowl and whisk together until the mixture is thick and pale and forms ribbons when the whisk is lifted, then beat in the cream cheese. Stir in the chocolate mixture and fold in the chopped nuts.

6 Pour the filling into the prepared case and bake in the oven for 2 hours. Leave to cool then chill in the fridge (it will sink in the centre).

7 Before serving, remove from the tin. Whip the cream until it stands in soft peaks then use to decorate the cheesecake with the pecan nuts.

CHOCOLATE AND CHESTNUT TORTE

This torte is rich but not too sweet. I like to serve it with ginger ice cream and seasonal fruits.

SERVES 6

25 g (1 oz) soft plain white flour, plus extra for
   dusting
100 g (4 oz) bitter couverture chocolate or
   good, high percentage cocoa butter chocolate
100 g (4 oz) butter
4 large eggs
300 g (11 oz) canned, sweetened chestnut puree
1 teaspoon natural vanilla essence
⅛ teaspoon cream of tartar
50 g (2 oz) caster sugar
icing sugar, for dusting

1 Preheat the oven to 180C (350F/Gas 4). Grease and line a 20 cm (8 in) deep round cake tin. Dust with flour.

2 Break the chocolate into a bowl, and add the butter. Place over a saucepan of simmering water, stirring occasionally, until smooth. Take care not to overheat.

3 Separate the eggs. Sift the flour into a bowl, add the egg yolks, chestnut puree, vanilla and flour and whisk together. Stir in the chocolate mixture.

4 Whisk egg whites and cream of tartar until soft peaks form, then gradually whisk in sugar until stiff. Do not overbeat.

5 Fold a quarter of the egg whites into the chocolate mixture, then the remaining whites.

6 Pour into the prepared tin and bake in the oven for 40–45 minutes, until a skewer inserted into the centre comes out moist but not sticky. Leave the torte to cool in the tin on a rack. It will have risen and then dropped slightly in the centre, so level with a palette knife.

7 When cold, turn out and dust with sifted icing sugar.

• During cooking, the torte puffs up like a souffle but then sinks in the centre when left to cool. Don't worry – it's supposed to! The torte should be stored at room temperature and is best if made at least one day in advance. It can be frozen and kept for up to three months.

BLACK GRAPE CAKE WITH OLIVE OIL

This cake should be made when black grapes are at their best – end of September, beginning October. Baking grapes in a batter is unusual but the result is a moist, sweet cake.

SERVES 8

225 g (8 oz) plain white or '00' Italian flour, plus a little extra for dusting

450 g (1 lb) seedless sweet black grapes

150 g (5 oz) golden caster sugar

1 teaspoon baking powder

3 large eggs

3 tablespoons extra virgin olive oil

icing sugar, for dusting (optional)

1 Preheat the oven to 200C (400F/Gas 6). Grease a deep, round 20 cm (8 in) cake tin.

Dust with flour. Dust the grapes with a little flour.

2 Put the flour, sugar and baking powder in a large bowl. Add the eggs, one at a time, beating well after each addition, until the mixture is the consistency of batter. Add the grapes and the olive oil and mix well together.

3 Pour the mixture into the prepared tin and bake for about 50 minutes, until golden and well risen.

4 Turn out the cake and leave to cool on a wire rack. When cool, dust the top of the cake with sifted icing sugar, if liked.

• This cake is best eaten within 2 days but it freezes very successfully.

DRIED PLUM GNOCCHI WITH CLOVES

This is another example of my love of prunes and how tasty and versatile they can be.

SERVES 4

14 dried prunes

900 g (2 lb) floury potatoes

275 (10 oz) plain white flour

1 egg

salt

90 g (3 oz) butter

90 g (3 oz) fresh breadcrumbs

pinch of freshly ground cloves

1 Soak the prunes in water for 4 hours or overnight, to soften. Drain and pit them. Cut into small pieces.

2 Cook the potatoes in their skins in boiling water for about 20 minutes, until tender.

Peel then push through a sieve into a bowl. Add two-thirds of the flour, the egg and salt.

3 Knead the potato mixture well. Form into balls the size of a chestnut and place a piece of prune in each gnocchi. Arrange on a floured board.

4 Bring a large saucepan of salted water to the boil. Cook the gnocchi, a few at a time. Wait until they bob to the top, count to 30 then remove with a slotted spoon. Arrange on a warmed serving dish and keep warm.

5 Melt the butter in a saucepan. Add the breadcrumbs and cloves and fry until golden. Drizzle over the cooked gnocchi and serve.

• Prunes tend to be sticky, so I suggest you use scissors, dipped in flour, to cut them into small pieces.

Top to bottom: *Black grape cake with olive oil; Dried plum gnocchi with cloves.*

HOT SPICED BANANAS WITH AMARETTO CREAM

I think bananas are a super food. They literally unzip and are ready for eating – you then have an instant, nutritious snack. I love the smell and taste and eat one every day. At the Cordon Vert Cookery school, my assistant often hides them from me, as many times I've been carried away and eaten some reserved for the next day's recipes!

SERVES 4

1 wine glass of white wine

2 cinnamon sticks, about 10 cm (4 in) long

100 g (4 oz) muscovado sugar

12 cloves

300 ml (½ pint) pineapple juice

freshly grated nutmeg

4 bananas

150 ml (¼ pint) double cream

1 teaspoon amaretto liqueur

1 In a large saucepan, combine the wine, cinnamon sticks, sugar, cloves, pineapple juice and a pinch of nutmeg and boil the mixture for 5 minutes or until thickened slightly.

2 Cut the bananas in half lengthways. Add the banana halves to the pan and simmer the mixture for 5 minutes, turning the bananas once.

3 Meanwhile, whip the cream until stiff then fold in the amaretto and a pinch of nutmeg.

4 Using a slotted spoon, transfer the bananas to a serving dish. Spoon the sauce over them and serve the bananas with the whipped cream.

• Muscovado sugar is made from raw cane sugar and you can buy light and dark varieties. Light muscovado is pale golden with a fudge-like flavour. Dark muscovado contains more molasses and is therefore more moist and has a stronger flavour. If you use dark muscovado you will probably prefer to reduce the quantity.

DATE AND COGNAC ICE CREAM

A rich, naturally sweet ice-cream with a wonderful flavour. Look out for Medjool dates which are plump and full of flavour.

SERVES 4

175 g (6 oz) fresh dates

3 tablespoons Cognac

1 vanilla pod

500 ml (18 fl oz) whipping cream

250 ml (9 fl oz) milk

5 large egg yolks

100 g (4 oz) caster sugar

1 Stone the dates then finely chop the flesh and put in a bowl. Add the Cognac and leave to marinate in the fridge overnight.

2 The next day, put the split vanilla pod in a saucepan with the cream and milk. Bring to the boil, remove from the heat and leave to infuse for 15 minutes.

3 In a separate bowl, whisk together the egg yolks and sugar until thick and cream. Stir into the cream then whisk over a medium heat until nearly boiling, then pour over the dates and stir well together. Leave to cool then chill in the fridge for 2-3 hours or preferably overnight.

4 Remove the vanilla pod and freeze the mixture for 2 hours. Beat well then spoon into a container and freeze until firm.

• Don't discard the vanilla pod after using it to flavour the milk, wash and dry well and use again.

FRAGRANT ALMOND CAKE

Fresh almonds are my favourite nuts and used in this recipe, make a moist cake.

SERVES 6

40 g (1½ oz) butter
50 g (2 oz) plain white flour
50 g (2 oz) potato flour
pinch of ground cinnamon
pinch of ground allspice
grated rind of 1 lemon
4 eggs
75 g (3 oz) caster sugar
50 g (2 oz) ground almonds
2 tablespoons amaretto
75 g (3 oz) plain chocolate

1 Grease and line an 18 cm (7 in) deep round cake tin. Preheat the oven to 180C (350F/Gas 4).

2 Melt the butter. Sift the plain flour, potato flour, cinnamon and allspice into a bowl. Add the lemon rind.

3 Separate the eggs. Add sugar to yolks and whisk until light and frothy. Fold in the flour mixture, melted butter, almonds and amaretto.

4 Whisk the egg whites until stiff, then carefully fold into the mixture.

5 Spoon into tin. Bake for about 1 hour, until well risen. Cool on a rack.

7 Break chocolate into a bowl and add 1 tablespoon of water. Place over a saucepan of simmering water, stirring, until smooth. Spread over cake and leave to set.

• Potato flour is the fine, soft, white starch extracted from potatoes after pulverizing and washing. It gives cakes a dry, light texture and is available from health food shops.

DRIED PEARS, PEACHES AND FIGS IN RED WINE

This is a wonderful winter fruit salad. Serve with cream or ice cream.

SERVES 6

100 g (4 oz) dried pears
100 g (4 oz) dried peaches
100 g (4 oz) dried figs
300 ml (½ pint) red wine
175 g (6 oz) caster sugar
2-3 pieces pared lemon rind
1 cinnamon stick

1 Put the dried pears, peaches and figs in a large bowl, cover with cold water and leave to soak overnight. The next day, drain and separate the figs.

2 Put the red wine, 200 ml (½ pint) water and the sugar into a large saucepan. Add the pared lemon rind and cinnamon stick and stir over a low heat to dissolve the sugar.

3 Add the figs and simmer for 10 minutes. Add the pears and peaches and cook for a further 20–30 minutes or until tender.

4 Transfer fruits to a serving bowl. Bring syrup to the boil and simmer for 2–3 minutes.

5 Remove from heat, discard lemon peel and cinnamon stick and pour hot syrup over fruits. Leave to cool, before serving.

• Look for a variety of good dried fruits in your local health store.

Clockwise from top:
*Pecan meringue cake
with caramelised
apples; Baked
peaches with
amaretti, Zesty
souffles with apricot
sauce.*

ZESTY SOUFFLÉS WITH APRICOT SAUCE

These chilled individual soufflés are very light and fresh. They look delicate so I like to serve them at a summer luncheon party.

SERVES 6

3 eggs, separated

1 tablespoon vanilla sugar

100 g (3½ oz) fromage frais

grated rind of ½ a lemon

75 g (3 oz) caster sugar

450 g (1 lb) apricots

125 g (4 oz) sugar

juice of 1 lemon

4 tablespoons Muscat wine

6 sprigs of fresh mint, to decorate

1 Butter 6 individual ramekin dishes. Preheat the oven to 220C (425F/Gas 7).

2 Whisk the egg yolks with the vanilla sugar until thick and pale. Add the fromage frais and lemon rind and mix well together.

Whisk the egg whites until they stand in stiff peaks, add the caster sugar and whisk until very thick and glossy. Fold into the egg yolk mixture.

3 Pour the mixture into the prepare ramekin dishes. Place the ramekins in a roasting tin and add boiling water so that it comes halfway up the sides of the dishes. Bake for 20 minutes. Remove from oven, allow to cool, then chill thoroughly.

4 Meanwhile, make the sauce. Remove stones from apricots and cut flesh into pieces. Put in a pan with the sugar, lemon juice and wine and cook gently for 10 minutes until tender. Purée in a blender or food processor and chill.

5 To serve, unmould the soufflés on to individual serving plates and surround with apricot sauce. Decorate with mint sprigs.

• Dried apricots may be used in the sauce if fresh ones are not around. Use 225 g (8 oz); soak overnight in cold water then cook for 30 minutes until tender.

BAKED PEACHES WITH AMARETTI

SERVES 6

6 yellow peaches

25 g (1 oz) butter

6 Amaretti (almond macaroons)

1 egg yolk

2 tablespoons maraschino, Marsala or Amaretto almond liqueur

50 g (2 oz) finely chopped almonds

100 g (4 oz) sugar

1 teaspoon cocoa powder

grated rind of ½ a lemon

150 ml (¼ pint) white wine

50 g (2 oz) caster sugar

50 g (2 oz) butter

1 Preheat the oven to 180C (350F/Gas 4). Cut the peaches in half, ease out the stones and hollow out some of the flesh. Chop the flesh. Crush macaroons and mix together with the egg yolks, maraschino, almonds, sugar, cocoa and lemon rind.

2 Fill the peach halves with this mixture and arrange in a buttered oven dish. Sprinkle with white wine, dust with half the sugar and put a shaving of butter on each.

3 Bake in the oven for 20–30 minutes, until golden. Serve dusted with remaining sugar.

PECAN MERINGUE CAKE WITH CARAMELISED APPLES

I like to make the meringue 2-3 days in advance and serve this dessert at smart dinner parties.

SERVES 6 – 8

125 g (4 oz) caster sugar

150 g (5 oz) light muscovado sugar

125 g (4 oz) pecan nuts

4 large egg whites

2 teaspoons ground cinnamon

700 g (1½ lb) cooking apples

grated rind and juice of 1 lemon

450 g (1 lb) eating apples

50 g (2 oz) butter

300 ml (½ pint) double cream

150 ml (¼ pint) fromage frais

icing sugar and cinnamon, for dusting

1 Line 2 baking trays with non-stick baking parchment and draw a 20 cm (11 in) circle on each. Preheat the oven to 150C (300F/ Gas 2).

2 Sift together the caster sugar and 125 g (4 oz) muscovado sugar. Roughly chop the nuts.

3 Put the egg whites in a large bowl and whisk until stiff but not dry. Gradually whisk in the mixed sugars, 1 level tablespoon at a time, keeping the meringue mixture smooth and shiny. Gently fold in three-quarters of the chopped pecan nuts and the ground cinnamon.

4 Using two dessert spoons, and shaping the meringue into ovals, arrange about 16 ovals in a ring around one of the circles on the baking sheet. Sprinkle with remaining chopped nuts. Spread the remaining meringue into a round on the second baking sheet.

5 Bake in the oven for 1½ hours until crisp and dry. Transfer to a wire rack to cool, then carefully peel off the paper.

6 Meanwhile, peel, core and roughly chop the cooking apples. Put in a saucepan with grated lemon rind and juice and 50 ml (2 fl oz) water. Simmer for 10 minutes, until soft.

7 Peel, core and cut eating apples into 2.5 cm (1 in) slices. Melt the butter and remaining 25 g (1 oz) sugar in a frying pan. Add the apples and fry gently for 5 minutes, until they caramelise. Using a slotted spoon, transfer apples to a sheet of foil. Remove remaining caramel from the heat.

8 To assemble, spoon the apple sauce over the meringue round. Lightly whisk cream and fold in fromage frais. Spoon over the sauce. Place the meringue on top and fill the centre with caramelised apple slices. Spoon over any remaining caramel. Dust with a little sifted icing sugar and cinnamon.

• You can use any variety of eating apple for this recipe but my favourites are Braeburn and Cox's.

Cooking for Pleasure

*T*here are times when I don't cook out of necessity but simply because I

enjoy it. This chapter includes recipes which are my personal favourites.

There are several of my best bread recipes which are not only wonderful to

eat but therapeutic to make. Then there are little jars of things which are

lovely to have in the cupboard or the fridge – preserves, pickles and pestos.

They are fun to make and many of them make lovely gifts.

RUSTIC WALNUT BREAD

I love this bread, particularly if the walnuts are fresh and it is served with a strong cheese. The combination is very good indeed! It is excellent for sandwiches or mopping up the juices from a gratin or the dressing from a salad.

MAKES 1 LARGE OR 2 MEDIUM LOAVES

125 g (4 oz) walnut pieces

1 teaspoon fennel seeds

600 g (1 lb 6 oz) strong white unbleached flour

1 teaspoon salt

25 g (1 oz) butter

15 g (½ oz) fresh yeast or 1½ teaspoons dried
   yeast and a pinch of sugar

1 Roughly chop the walnuts. Crush the fennel seeds. Sift the flour and salt into a warmed large mixing bowl. Rub in the butter until mixture resembles bread-crumbs. Stir in fennel seeds and walnuts.

2 Cream together the fresh yeast and 350 ml (12 fl oz) hand-hot water. (If using dried yeast, sprinkle it into 350 ml (12 fl oz) hand-hot water with the sugar and leave in a warm place for 15 minutes until frothy.)

3 Add yeast mixture to flour and, using a wooden spoon, mix to a smooth ball of dough, adding more water if necessary.

4 Turn the dough on to a work surface and knead for 10 minutes, until smooth.

5 Either divide the dough in 2 or keep as 1 large loaf. Shape into a round and place on an oiled baking tray. Cover with a clean damp tea-towel and leave to rise for about 1 hour, until it has doubled in size.

6 Preheat the oven to 220C (425F/Gas 7). Slash top of dough with a sharp knife and bake for 10 minutes. Reduce temperature to 190C (375F/Gas 5) and bake for a further 20 minutes, until bread sounds hollow when tapped on the bottom. If the bread becomes too dark, cover with foil during cooking. Turn out and cool on a rack.

• For bread rolls, divide the dough into about 18 pieces, shape into balls, leave to rise until doubled in size and then bake in the oven at 220C (425F/Gas 7) for 15 to 20 minutes. Great with blue cheese and young spinach leaves for sandwiches.

SOUR DOUGH BREAD

For me, this is the ultimate in bread dough for flavour. However, it does take time but it is worth it. At the Cordon Vert cookery school, where I teach, it is voted the best bread and once the students have tried it they are all converted. I hope you will be too.

MAKES 2 LOAVES

15 g (½ oz) fresh yeast or 1½ teaspoons dried
   yeast and a pinch of sugar

1.15 g (2 lb 6 oz) strong white unbleached flour

1 tablespoon salt

1 To make the starter, cream the fresh yeast with 90 ml (3½ fl oz) hand-hot water. (If using dried yeast, sprinkle it into 90 ml (3½ fl oz) hand-hot water and leave in a warm place for 15 minutes until frothy.) Add 100 g (4 oz) flour and mix together. Cover and leave for 24 hours, during which time the starter will expand and ferment.

2 The next day, add 120 ml (4 fl oz) hand-hot water and 175 g (6 oz) flour and mix well together. The mixture should be slack,

• To the dough (step 3) you can add up to 175 g (6 oz) additional ingredients such as gorgonzola cheese and stoned black olives.

if not add a little more water. Leave for a further 24 hours.

3 The following day, add 425 ml (15 fl oz) hand-hot water, salt and remaining 875 g (1¾ lb) flour and mix together. Knead well for 10 minutes, adding more flour, if necessary.

4 Put the dough in a bowl, cover with a clean tea-towel and leave to rise in a warm place for 1½ hours, until double in size.

5 Knead dough for 3 minutes. Cover and leave to rise again for a further 1½ hours.

6 Knock back for a second time. Knead for 3 minutes, cut the dough in half and shape into 2 large ovals. Place on a baking tray, slash the tops 3 times and dust with flour. Leave to rise for 20 minutes.

7 Preheat the oven to 200C (400F/Gas 6). Place a roasting tin of water in the oven (it will give the bread an excellent crust) and bake for 45 minutes, until golden brown and sounds hollow when tapped on the bottom. Turn out and cool on a wire rack.

FOCACCIA

This flat bread, found throughout Italy, varies from region to region by the addition of a simple seasoned topping. This one is topped with crushed garlic and rosemary and is my favourite. It is traditionally eaten as a snack.

MAKES 1 LOAF

15 g (½ oz) fresh yeast or 1½ teaspoons dried
   yeast and a pinch of sugar
225 g (8 oz) strong white unbleached flour
salt
3-4 tablespoons olive oil
1 garlic clove
2 teaspoons dried rosemary

1 Cream the fresh yeast with 3 tablespoons hand-hot water. (If using dried yeast, sprinkle it into 3 tablespoons hand-hot water with the sugar and leave in a warm place for 15 minutes until frothy.)

2 Put the flour on a clean working surface. Gently mix in 1 teaspoon salt, then form into a mound with a hollow in the centre.

3 Pour the yeast liquid into the hollow and carefully fold the flour over it, then add 3 tablespoons olive oil. Add about 100ml (4 fl oz) hand-hot water to make a stiff but pliable dough. Knead for 10-15 minutes.

4 Put the dough in a bowl and cover with a clean tea-towel. Leave in a warm place for about 30 minutes, until doubled in size.

5 Preheat the oven to 220C (425F/Gas 7). On a lightly floured surface, roll out the dough to a round about 0.5 cm (¼ in) thick.

6 Brush a baking tray with some of the olive oil and place the dough on the tray. Crush the garlic, put in a bowl and add some more of the oil. Brush on to the dough and sprinkle with salt and rosemary.

7 Bake for 10 minutes, then reduce heat to 190C (375F/Gas 5) and bake for a further 20 minutes. Serve hot.

• **As a variation, you can use chopped sage instead of rosemary.**

Clockwise from top: *Focaccia; Rustic walnut bread; Sour dough bread wih gorgonzola and olives; Grissini.*

GRISSINI

These breadsticks are not difficult to make and look fabulous served with soups and antipasti.

MAKES 24

15 g (½oz) fresh yeast or 1½ teaspoons dried
  yeast and a pinch of sugar

275 g (10 oz) strong white unbleached flour or
  strong brown (wheatmeal) flour

1 teaspoon salt

2 tablespoons extra virgin olive oil

1 egg

50 g (2 oz) sesame seeds

1 Cream together the fresh yeast and 3 tablespoons hand-hot water. (If using dried yeast, sprinkle it into 3 tablespoons hand-hot water with the sugar and leave in a warm place for 15 minutes until frothy.)

2 Sift the flour and salt into a large bowl. Add oil, yeast liquid and 150 ml (¼ pint) hand-hot water and mix to a soft dough, adding more water if necessary.

3 Knead for 3–4 minutes, until smooth and elastic. Cover with a clean tea-towel and leave for 10 minutes. Knead for 3 minutes then divide into 24 equal pieces.

4 Roll each piece into a sausage shape the thickness of your little finger. Place on oiled baking trays and leave to rise for 15 minutes.

5 Preheat the oven to 150C (300F/Gas 2). Beat egg and brush over the dough. Sprinkle with sesame seeds and bake for 45 minutes, until brown. Cool on a wire rack.

• Grissini can be kept in an airtight container for up to 2 weeks.

POTATO PIZZA BREAD

Serve this bread with soup.

SERVES 4

275 g (10 oz) even sized old potatoes

50 g (2 oz) freshly grated Parmesan cheese

1 teaspoon freshly grated nutmeg

25 g (1 oz) fresh yeast or 1 tablespoon dried
  yeast and 1 teaspoon sugar

900 g (2 lb) plain white unbleached flour

salt

1 tablespoon olive oil

1 Cook the potatoes in their skins in boiling water for about 20 minutes, until tender. Drain and when cool enough to handle, peel then mash. Add cheese and nutmeg.

2 Blend yeast with 4 tablespoons hand-hot water. (If using dried yeast, sprinkle it into the water with the sugar and leave in a warm place for 15 minutes until frothy.)

3 Spread potato on to a work surface. Add flour, salt, yeast mixture and gradually add about 250 ml (8fl oz) hand-hot water to give a smooth dough. Knead for 5–10 minutes.

4 Put the dough on an oiled baking tray. Flatten into a 25 cm (10 in) round. Leave to rise for 1 hour, until doubled in size.

5 Preheat the oven to 200C (400F/Gas 6). Sprinkle the pizza with the oil and bake in the oven for 40 minutes, until golden brown. Serve warm.

• Choose a good mashing potato like a Kind Edward or a Desiree. Don't be tempted to mash the potatoes in a food processor – they go gluey.

FLATTENED BREAD FILLED WITH SPINACH AND OLIVES

This bread encloses a filling of spinach and olives, seasoned with garlic and chilli, like a large parcel. It is a delicious lunch or supper meal served with a salad, or a great picnic bread.

MAKES ONE 33cm (13in) LOAF

Dough

2 tablespoons olive oil plus extra for drizzling on
  top

500 g (1 lb) strong white unbleached flour

7 g (¼ oz) fresh yeast or 1 teaspoon dried yeast
  and a pinch of sugar

1 teaspoon salt

Filling

1 large red onion

1 garlic clove

½ dried red chilli

750 g (1½ lb) fresh tender spinach

1 tablespoon olive oil

125 g (4 oz) stoned black olives

3 tablespoons freshly grated Parmesan

coarse sea salt and pepper

1 To prepare the dough, cream the yeast with 300 ml (10 fl oz) hand-hot water. (If using dried yeast, sprinkle it into 300 ml (10 fl oz) hand-hot water with sugar and leave in a warm place for 15 minutes until frothy.)

2 Put the flour and salt in a large bowl. Make a reservoir in the centre with a wooden spoon and add the oil and yeast liquid. Mix well together adding more water if necessary to form a soft, springy dough.

3 Turn out on to a lightly floured surface

and knead for 10 minutes until smooth and elastic.

4 Put in a clean bowl, cover with a clean damp tea-towel and leave to rise in a warm place for about 1 hour, until it has doubled in size.

5 Meanwhile, prepare the filling. Slice the onion and crush the garlic and red chilli. Wash the spinach well and chop roughly, discarding any coarse stalks. Heat the oil in a saucepan, add the onion and cook for about 5 minutes until soft. Add the garlic and chilli and cook for 1 minute. Add spinach and olives and cook until spinach just begins to wilt. Remove from the heat and stir in the cheese. Season with salt and pepper.

6 When risen, turn the dough on to a lightly floured surface and knead to knock out the air bubbles. Divide the dough in half and roll out each half to a 33 cm (13 in) round.

7 Place one round on a greased baking tray. Spread the filling over the round. Dampen the edge and place the remaining dough round on top. Pinch the edges together to seal.

8 Leave to rise in a warm place for 20–30 minutes, until doubled in size.

9 Preheat the oven to 200C (400F/Gas 6). Brush the dough with oil and sprinkle with salt. Bake in the oven for about 25 minutes until golden brown. Serve hot, warm or cold.

• You can vary the fillings of this flattened bread to suit your taste. Try a simple filling of onion flavoured with fresh herbs, or your favourite pizza topping would make a good filling.

PRUNE AND CHOCOLATE BREAD

I adore prunes and wish they were taken more seriously. They are an excellent source of Vitamin A with iron and fibre. The combination of prunes and chocolate is heavenly. This is a wonderful breakfast bread – it is rich, sweet, dark and delicious and doesn't need anything else with it. Try it with half dark chocolate, half good quality white chocolate too.

MAKES TWO 900 g (2 lb) LOAVES

20 g (¾oz) fresh yeast or 1 tablespoon dried
　　yeast and 1 teaspoon sugar
750 g (1½ lb) strong white unbleached flour or
　　half strong white and half strong wholemeal
　　flour
2 teaspoons salt
375 g (12 oz) stoned prunes
375 g (12 oz) plain chocolate
20 g (¾ oz) butter
1 egg

1 Grease two 900 g (2 lb) loaf tins, two 450 g (1 lb) loaf tins or a baking tray. Blend the fresh yeast with 450 ml (¾ pint) hand-hot water. (If using dried yeast, sprinkle it into the hand-hot water with the sugar and leave in a warm place for 15 minutes until frothy.)

2 Mix the flour and salt together well. Make a reservoir in the centre with a wooden spoon.

3 Gradually add about ¾ of the yeast liquid to the flour and mix well together. (I find that different flours absorb different amounts of liquid, so I never add all the liquid at once). The dough should be firm and leave the sides of the bowl clean. If it looks dry, add some of the remaining yeast liquid.

4 Now lightly flour the work surface and turn the dough out. Knead well for 10 minutes – you should end up with a smooth, elastic dough.

5 Return your dough to a clean bowl, cover with a clean tea-towel and leave to rise somewhere warm and free of draughts for 1 hour, until doubled in size. Meanwhile, chop the prunes, chocolate and butter. Beat the egg.

6 Turn the dough back on to a lightly floured work surface and knead again to knock out the air bubbles. It will return to its original size. Add the prunes, chocolate, butter and beaten egg and knead well for 10 minutes. You may need a little extra flour if the mixture is tacky.

7 Divide and put dough in the prepared tins or shape into ovals and place on the baking tray. Allow to rise for 10 minutes.

8 Meanwhile, preheat the oven to 220C (425F/Gas 7). Bake the loaves for 35 minutes. The bread will be ready when, if turned out of the tin and tapped on the base, it sounds hollow.

9 Leave to cool on a wire rack. Serve warm – the chocolate should be melted and the prunes juicy.

• **When you are kneading bread dough, stand one foot in front of the other and let your body sway backwards and forwards. This is such good exercise and once you are in a rhythm, very soothing.**

Top to bottom: *Prune and chocolate bread; Amaretti.*

AMARETTI

The almond macaroons are the perfect partner for espresso coffee. They are very easy to make yourself.

MAKES 24
225 g (8 oz) ground almonds
225 g (8 oz) caster sugar
3 egg whites
1 teapoon almond essence (optional)

1 Dust baking trays with flour or line with rice paper. Put the sugar and almonds in a bowl and mix together.

2 In a large bowl, whisk the egg whites until stiff but not dry. Gradually fold in the almond mixture and add the almond essence, if using.

3 Pipe or spoon the mixture on to the prepared baking trays. Leave for as long as possible to rest before baking.

4 Preheat the oven to 180C (350F/Gas 4). Bake in the oven for 20 minutes, until golden brown. They should be crisp on the outside but with a rather chewy centre. Longer cooking will crisp them all the way through if liked. Transfer to a wire rack and leave to cool.

• They will keep for up to 1 week in an airtight container. When cold, wrap in pairs in twists of coloured tissue paper and pack into boxes for presents.

HOME-MADE TOASTED ALMOND BUTTER

Made with almonds, this is my favourite butter which I spread on toast or stir into pasta and rice dishes. Like peanut butter, it can be made crunchy or smooth by running the food processor accordingly.

MAKES 225 g (8 oz)
225 g (8 oz) whole blanched almonds
1-3 teaspoons peanut or groundnut oil
salt (optional)

1 Preheat the oven to 180C (350F/Gas 4). Put the nuts on a baking tray and toast in the oven for 12 minutes, until golden.

2 Put the toasted nuts in a food processor and blend for 1 minute. Scrape the nuts off the sides of the processor bowl and continue blending for a further 1-2 minutes. Suddenly the nuts will become thicker – add some oil at this stage and continue to blend until you have a thick mixture, suitable for spreading.

3 Season with salt if wished. Pour the butter into a small, sterilized jar and cover. Store in the fridge and use within 2 weeks.

• You can make cashew, hazelnut and, of course, peanut butter. Each nut lends its own special character to the spread. Toasting the nuts gives them more flavour.

SWEET MILK BREAD WITH CUMIN AND ORANGE

This bread is aromatic and delicious. A wholemeal loaf enriched with butter, sweetened with soft brown sugar and honey and given a shiny glaze. Eat fresh with fresh fruit spread or toast and eat warm with butter.

MAKES TWO 900 g (2 lb) LOAVES

300 ml (10 fl oz) milk

25 g (1 oz) fresh yeast or 1 tablespoon dried
  yeast and 1 teaspoon sugar

175 g (6 oz) unsalted butter

50 g (2 oz) soft brown sugar

50 g (2 oz) honey plus 2 tablespoons, to glaze

2 teaspoons salt

75 ml (3 fl oz) fresh orange juice

1 egg

500 g (1 lb) strong wholemeal flour

1 tablespoon cumin seed

415 g (14½ oz) strong white flour

1 Grease two 900 g (2 lb) loaf tins. Bring the milk almost to boiling point then remove from the heat and leave until hand-hot.

2 Cream the fresh yeast with the milk. (If using dried yeast, sprinkle it into the milk with the sugar and leave in a warm place for 15 minutes until frothy.)

3 In a large bowl, cream together 150 g (5 oz) of the butter, the sugar and honey until well blended. Add the salt and gradually stir in the yeast liquid.

4 Beat the egg. Add to the milk mixture with the orange juice and mix well together. Beat in the wholemeal flour, the cumin seeds and three-quarters of the white flour until well mixed.

5 Turn on to a lightly flour work surface and knead for 10 minutes, incorporating enough of the remaining flour to form a soft dough.

6 Put the dough in a large buttered bowl, cover with a damp clean tea-towel and leave to rise in a warm place for about 1 hour, until it has doubled in size.

7 Turn the dough on to a lightly floured surface and knead for 1 minute to knock out the air bubbles. Grease the bowl again, cover and leave to rise for 30 minutes.

8 Divide the dough in half, knead again and place in the prepared loaf tins. Leave to rise for 30 minutes or until they have risen just above the tops of the tins.

9 Preheat the oven to 220C (425F/Gas 7). Bake the loaves for 10 minutes. Reduce the temperature to 190C (375F/Gas 5) and bake for a further 25-30 minutes, until golden and sounds hollow when tapped on the bottom.

10 Meanwhile, make the glaze. Cream together the remaining 25 g (1 oz) butter and the honey. When the loaves are cooked, turn out on to a wire rack. Whilst the loaves are still hot, brush the tops with the glaze then leave to cool completely.

• Although the loaves will keep fresh for about 2 days, it is a good idea to freeze one of the loaves for later. Any loaf not eaten fresh can be turned into a wonderful bread and butter pudding.

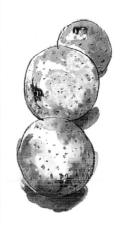

RUM PLUM BREAD

I sometimes feel like something sweet for lunch or a snack. This plum bread, made without yeast, usually fits the bill. It's a fruity tealoaf with lemon and spices and, of course, rum – and is very moreish!

MAKES TWO 900 g (2 lb) LOAVES
750 g (1½ lb) white or wholemeal self raising flour
1 teaspoon salt
2 teaspoons ground mixed spice
grated rind of 1 lemon
225 g (8 oz) unsalted butter
350 g (12 oz) muscovado sugar
4 eggs
450 ml (16 fl oz) milk
4 tablespoons dark rum
450 g (1 lb) prunes (preferably unsulphured and stoned)
225 g (8 oz) raisins
450 g (1 lb) sultanas

1 Preheat the oven to 170C (325F/Gas 3).

Butter two 23 × 125 × 5 cm (9 × 5 × 2 in) loaf tins and line the bases with parchment paper.

2 Sift flour, salt and mixed spice into a large bowl. Add lemon rind and cut the butter into the flour. Rub in with the fingertips until it resembles breadcrumbs. Seive in the sugar and mix in.

3 Break the eggs into a jug. Add the milk and rum and beat to mix.

4 Chop prunes with a knife dipped into flour and mix with the raisins and sultanas.

5 Add fruit and egg mixture to flour mixture and mix well.

6 Divide between the 2 tins and spread evenly. Bake for 2–2½ hours until firm to the touch. Turn out of the tins and leave to cool on a wire rack.

• **Rum plum bread is lovely toasted and spread with butter. The loaves will last for up to 1 month, if well wrapped.**

BRANDY, DATE AND ORANGE CREAM CHEESE

Perfect on scones, toast or fruity teabread and brilliant on brioche. The ingredients always feel quite Christmassy but I enjoy it all the year round.

MAKES ABOUT 350 g (12 oz)
125 g (4 oz) fresh dates
grated rind of 1 orange
225 g (8 oz) smooth, full fat soft cheese
1 teaspoon vanilla essence
1 teaspoon ground mixed spice
1 tablespoon brandy

1 Stone the dates then finely chop the flesh and put in a bowl.

2 Add the orange rind, soft cheese, vanilla essence, mixed spice and brandy and mix well together.

3 Turn into a bowl and serve or store in the fridge until required.

• **Store, covered, in the fridge for up to 1 week. The flavour develops on keeping.**

Clockwise from top: *Sweet milk bread with cumin and orange; Banana, date and orange cream cheese, Rum plum bread.*

Mrs ferrigno's featherlight walnut scones

This is my mother's recipe – I hope you will enjoy them. They are delicious served with sweet preserves or cheese.

MAKES 8

225 g (8 oz) self raising white flour

pinch of salt

50 g (2 oz) butter

1 large egg, beaten

25 g (1 oz) sugar

50 g (2 oz) walnut pieces

150 ml (¼ pint) milk

1 Preheat the oven to 220C (425F/Gas 7). Sift the flour and salt into a large bowl and rub in the butter until the mixture resembles fine breadcrumbs. Stir in the sugar and walnuts.

2 Make a well in the centre and stir in the beaten egg and enough milk to make a light spongy dough.

3 Turn on to a floured surface and knead very lightly, to remove cracks then roll out lightly to 2.5 cm (1 inch). Cut into rounds with a 5 cm (2 in) cutter (dipped in flour). Place on a lightly floured baking tray. Bake at the top of the oven for 7-10 minutes until browned and well risen. Transfer to a wire rack and leave to cool. Serve split and buttered.

• These scones are very versatile. You can add dates, dried fruit or a mixture of all.

Taralli

These are eaten throughout Southern Italy as an appetiser to be served with drinks. They are similar to a bagel but crunchy.

MAKES 20

25 g (1oz) fresh yeast or 1 tablespoon dried yeast and 1 teaspoon sugar

775 g (1¾ lb) strong white flour

2 tablespoons extra virgin olive oil

3 large eggs

2 teaspoons fennel seeds

salt and pepper

1 Blend the fresh yeast with 150 ml (¼ pint) hand-hot water. (If using dried yeast, sprinkle it into the water and leave in a warm place for 15 minutes until frothy.)

2 Put 225 g (8 oz) of the flour in a large bowl and make a hollow in the centre. Pour the yeast liquid into the well, mix with a wooden spoon, incorporating half of the flour. Cover the bowl with a clean tea towel and leave in a warm place for 1 hour, until doubled in size.

3 Put the remaining 550 g (1¼ lb) of flour in a mound on a clean work surface and make a hollow in the centre.

4 Put the yeast mixture in the hollow with the remaining unincorporated flour. Add the oil, 2 of the eggs, fennel seeds, 1 teaspoon salt and pepper.

5 Mix together all the ingredients in the hollow, then start incorporating the flour from the inside edge of the hollow. Keep

• They keep for up to 1 month in an airtight tin and children love them.

mixing until all but 5 tablespoons of the flour is incorporated. Knead for 5 minutes.

6 Cut the dough into four pieces. Using the four fingers of both hands, lightly roll each piece until 63 cm (25 in) long. Divide into 5 equal pieces, then take each piece and connect the two ends together to form a circle. Leave to rest for 15 minutes.

7 Preheat the oven to 200C (400F/Gas 6). Lightly oil 2 baking trays.

CIABATTA

Literally, Ciabatta means slipper because that's what these crisp, open-textured flat Italian breads look like. It is worth the effort!

MAKES 2 SMALL LOAVES

Sponge

7 g (¼ oz) fresh yeast or 1 teaspoon dried yeast and a pinch of sugar

150 ml (¼ pt) warm milk

1 teaspoon honey or sugar

500 g (1 lb) strong white unbleached flour

Dough

7 g (¼ oz) fresh yeast or 1 teaspoon dried yeast and a pinch of sugar

1 tablespoon salt

3 tablespoons extra virgin olive oil

1.1 kg (2½ lb) strong white unbleached flour

1 To prepare the sponge: cream the fresh yeast with 350 ml (12 fl oz) hand–hot water. (If using dried yeast, sprinkle it into the water with the sugar and leave in a warm place for 15 minutes until frothy).

2 Stir in the milk, honey or sugar and flour and whisk together to form a batter. Cover

8 Fill a large saucepan or flameproof casserole with water and bring to the boil. When boiling, add salt, and then put in 4 or 5 Taralli and boil for 30 seconds. Remove with a slotted spoon, allow to drain well then place on the baking trays. Continue until all the Taralli have been boiled.

9 Brush with the remaining beaten egg and bake in the oven for 30 minutes until golden brown. Transfer to a wire rack and leave to cool.

loosely with a clean tea-towel and leave overnight at room temperature.

3 To make the dough: cream the fresh yeast, with 475 ml (16 fl oz) hand-hot water. (If using dried yeast, sprinkle it into the water with the sugar and leave in a warm place for 15 minutes until frothy.)

4 Add the yeast liquid to the sponge with salt and oil. Beat the mixture hard with a whisk for 3 minutes. Add the flour. Knead vigorously for 5 minutes. Leave for 10 minutes then knead again.

5 Place dough in a bowl. Cover with a clean tea-towel and leave in a warm place for 3 hours until 3 times its size.

6 Divide the dough into two, knead into 2 rounds then flatten. Dust with flour. Leave for a further 3 hours to rise slightly.

7 Preheat oven to 220C (425F/Gas 7) then bake loaves for 20 minutes until golden.

• Either start preparing the dough early in the day to allow time for it to rise or put in the refrigerator before the second rising and continue the following day.

FLORENTINES

These are good to have when friends pop around for coffee and make lovely presents.

MAKES 12
100 g (4 oz) whole blanched almonds
100 g (4 oz) whole blanched hazelnuts
100 g (4 oz) Brazil nuts
225 g (8 oz) natural red glace cherries
100 g (4 oz) glace fruits, such as melon,
**　pineapple, papaya, orange and lemon**
50 g (2 oz) plain flour
½ teaspoon ground allspice
½ teaspoon freshly grated nutmeg
100 g (4 oz) caster sugar
100 g (4 oz) clear honey
50 g (2 oz) plain chocolate

1 Preheat the oven to 180C (350F/Gas 4). Grease a 23 cm (9 in) round cake tin and line with non-stick baking parchment.

2 Put the almonds, hazelnuts and Brazil nuts on a baking tray and toast in the oven for 10 minutes. Put in a mixing bowl. Wash the cherries, chop the glace fruits and add to the nuts.

3 Sift the flour, ground allspice and nutmeg over the glace fruit and nuts and mix well together.

4 In a saucepan, warm the sugar and honey together over a low heat, until the sugar has dissolved.

5 Add the honey mixture to the fruit mixture and stir together.

6 Turn the mixture into the prepared tin and level the top. Bake in the oven for 25-30 minutes. Leave to cool in the tin.

7 Break the chocolate into small pieces and melt in a pan over boiling water. Spread over the nut mixture in an even layer. When cold, cut into wedges to serve.

• **Use good quality dark chocolate or the best white chocolate you can afford.**

BANANA CURD

This makes a sweet, thick spread which is wonderful on bread, ice cream or pancakes.

MAKES ABOUT TWO 450 g (1 lb) JARS
4 large bananas
125 g (4 oz) butter
250 g (8 oz) caster sugar
grated rind and juice of 1 lemon
pinch of ground ginger or 1 teaspoon chopped
**　fresh ginger**
4 eggs

1 Put the bananas in a bowl and mash.

2 Melt butter in a saucepan, then add sugar, bananas, lemon rind and juice and ginger. Cook gently for 10 minutes.

3 Beat the eggs in a bowl, then gradually beat in 3 tablespoons of the banana mixture. Pour into the banana mixture, stirring. Cook gently, stirring constantly, for 10 minutes or until mixture coats the back of a wooden spoon. Do not boil.

4 Pour into hot, sterilized jars and cover. Store in fridge and eat within 10 days.

• **It's very important to cook the curd over a gently heat so that the eggs thicken to a thick, shiny mixture. Too hot and the eggs will scramble.**

Clockwise from top:
Mrs Ferrigno's featherlight walnut scones; Banana curd; Florentines.

FRESH EGG PASTA

This is my basic pasta recipe and I recommend that you make a large amount. The dough can be kept in the fridge in an airtight container for 2-3 days or frozen for 1 month. Try to find '00' Italian flour as this will give the best result.

SERVES 6-8

500 g (1 lb) flour '00' Italian or plain flour

5 eggs

salt

semolina, for sprinkling

1 Put the flour, eggs and a good pinch of salt in a food processor and mix until it forms a dough.

2 If using plain flour, put the dough in a polythene bag and refrigerate for at least 30 minutes before rolling out.

3 To shape: cut dough in two and cover one half with a polythene bag. Roll remaining half out to a rectangle. Roll out until almost paper thin, sprinkling the surface with semolina if it begins to stick. Carefully transfer the sheet of pasta to a clean tea-towel, which has been sprinkled with semolina. Leave to rest for about 1 hour. Do not allow the pasta to dry out too much. Repeat with the remaining dough.

4 Using a sharp knife or pastry wheel, cut the sheets of pasta into the required shapes. Spread cut pasta out on to a clean tea-towel. Use within 24 hours.

5 To cook: bring a large saucepan of salted water to the boil then add the pasta. Return to the boil and cook for 2-3 minutes. Drain and serve tossed in butter, with a sauce or according to individual recipes.

Varieties of fresh pasta
By adding extra ingredients, a variety of different flavoured and coloured pasta can be made.

Spinach pasta
Cook 225 g (8 oz) young tender spinach in only the water that clings to the leaves after washing, for 5 minutes until tender. Drain well, squeeze out the water and puree in a food processor. Add to the flour mixture.

Tomato pasta
Add 2 tablespoons sun dried tomato puree (see page 132) and 1 tablespoon chopped fresh herbs to the flour mixture.

Saffron pasta
Add a large pinch of saffron to the flour mixture.

• **The conditions for pasta making are important. Cool hands, cool work surface and, of course, a cool kitchen.**

SUN DRIED TOMATO PUREE

MAKES 225 g (8 oz)

225 g (8 oz) sun dried tomatoes preserved in oil

1 Put the tomatoes in a food processor and blend until smooth. Store in a jar, in the fridge and use when tomato puree is required in a recipe.

• **This puree is concentrated so use only a third of the usual amount.**

CORIANDER, MINT AND CHILLI CHUTNEY

This heavenly, fresh-tasting mixture can be added to roasted vegetables or served with Indian dishes.

MAKES ABOUT 225 g (8 oz)

1 garlic clove

1 large handful of fresh coriander

1 large handful of fresh mint

1 tablespoon chopped red chilli

1 teaspoon chopped fresh ginger root

2 tablespoons lemon juice

1 teaspoon cumin

1 teaspoon honey

100 ml (4 fl oz) natural yogurt

salt and pepper

1 Skin the garlic and put in a food processor. Add all the remaining ingredients, except the yogurt, salt and pepper, and mix well together. Stir in the yogurt and season with salt and pepper.

2 Turn into a bowl or jar, cover and store in the refrigerator for up to 4 days. Serve the chutney cold, with Indian dishes or added to roasted vegetables.

• Wear rubber gloves when chopping the chilli to prevent it from making your skin tingle.

FRAGRANT SALT

This is a Middle Eastern condiment. It has an appetising flavour which can be sprinkled on to almost everything.

MAKES 425 g (15 oz)

150 g (5 oz) sesame seeds

50 g (2 oz) coriander seeds

50 g (2 oz) cumin seeds

20 g (¾ oz) black peppercorns

65 g (2½ oz) whole blanched almonds

15 g (½ oz) dried mint

½ teaspoon cayenne

65 g (2½ oz) salt

1 Dry-fry the sesame seeds, coriander seeds, cumin seeds and peppercorns until warm, but not too hot then set aside.

2 In a food processor, blend the dry-fried spices for only 1–2 seconds, until broken. (If blended for too long they will turn into a paste). Transfer to a coffee grinder.

3 Blend the almonds in a food processor until finely chopped then add to the coffee grinder.

4 Add the mint, cayenne and salt and grind until all the ingredients are fine. Store in an airtight jar, in a cool place.

• This flavoured salt will last indefinitely.

PICKLED RED ONIONS

This is another all time favourite of mine. The rich colour of the onions in their spiced vinegar makes me think of glistening jewels. They are good in sandwiches, served with cheese or spring vegetables. I always have a jar of these in my cupboard.

MAKES SIX 350 g (12 oz) JARS
1.5 kg (3¼ lb) red onions
225 ml (8 fl oz) olive oil
225 g (8 oz) stoned prunes
200 ml (7 fl oz) red wine
350 g (12 oz) demerara sugar
250 ml (8 fl oz) sherry vinegar
salt and pepper
1½ teaspoons ground allspice

1 Peel and thinly slice the onions. Heat the oil in a frying pan and cook over a high heat for 5–6 minutes, stirring all the time, until the onions are softened. Reduce the heat and simmer for 40 minutes.

2 Chop the prunes and add to the pan with the red wine. Cook over a high heat until most of the liquid has evaporated. Then add the sugar and vinegar and reduce the heat again. Simmer the mixture until it thickens.

3 Remove from the heat and add 1 tablespoon salt, 1 tablespoon pepper and the allspice. Leave to cool.

4 When cold, pack into hot, sterilised jars and cover. Store the jars in a cool, dry, dark place.

• **Use any variety of red wine.**

PICKLED PUMPKIN

I first encountered this delicacy in Southern Italy. It is quite special and easy to make. Enjoy this pickled pumpkin in sandwiches, salads and as an accompaniment.

MAKES ABOUT ONE 450 g (1 lb) JAR
1 medium pumpkin, weighing about 1 kg (2 lb)
salt
2 garlic cloves
225 ml (8 fl oz) extra virgin olive oil
50 ml (2 fl oz) white wine vinegar
2 teaspoons dried thyme

1 Using a sharp knife, cut the pumpkin in half and scoop out the seeds. Cut into sections, remove the peel and chop the flesh into small cubes.

2 Bring a large saucepan of salted water to the boil. Add the pumpkin flesh and boil for 4 minutes, until tender but firm (it should still have a little bite in it). Drain, put in a large bowl and leave to cool.

3 When cold, chop the garlic and add to the pumpkin with the oil, vinegar and thyme. Mix well together then pack in a hot, sterilised jar and cover. Store in a cool, dry, dark place.

• **Don't waste the pumpkin seeds. They can be dried or roasted then peeled and eaten as a natural snack.**

Top to bottom:
Picked pumpkin;
Pickled aubergine;
Pickled red onions.

PICKLED AUBERGINES

My favourite way to eat these is with crusty bread but they are equally good on pizzas and in salads. They are one of the ingredients in my favourite sandwich, see page 21.

MAKES ONE 500 g (1 lb) JAR

2 medium aubergines

2-3 teaspoons freeze-dried oregano

1 tablespoon white wine vinegar

2 garlic cloves

225 ml (8 fl oz) extra virgin olive oil

1 Slice the aubergines into thin short strips, put in a colander and sprinkle with salt. Place a plate on top and weigh down. Leave for 30 minutes to extract the bitter juices.

2 Rinse the aubergine strips well and put in a saucepan of boiling salted water. Boil for 4 minutes. Drain and leave until cold.

3 When cold, add all the remaining ingredients to the aubergines and mix together.

4 Pack in a sterilised jar and cover. Leave for 1 month before use.

• **This pickle will last for up to 1 year so its worth making several jars at one time. In fact, its flavour improves with age.**

FRUITY OLIVE PATE

This is so quick to put together and keeps well in the fridge. Serve on good crusty bread.

MAKES ABOUT 225 g (8 oz)

175 g (6 oz) stoned black olives

2 garlic cloves

4 tablespoons fruity extra virgin olive oil

grated rind and juice of 1 lemon

pepper

handful of finely chopped fresh parsley

1 Finely chop the olives and garlic and put in a bowl. Add the oil, lemon rind and juice, pepper and parsley and mix well together to form a thick pate.

2 Put in a jar and store in the fridge for up to 3 weeks.

• **I like a coarse texture to this pate but if you prefer it smoother, I recommend you use a mortar and pestle or a food processor.**

LEMON GRASS OIL

This is good on salads or shaken on stir fries.

MAKES 550 ml (20 fl oz)

1 lemon grass stalk

1 garlic clove

500 ml (18 fl oz) extra virgin olive oil

4 bay leaves

2 peperoncino (dried red chillies)

3 peppercorns

1 Cut the lemon grass into 3 pieces. Peel the garlic.

2 Put in a jug and add the oil, bay leaves, peperoncino and peppercorns.

3 Pour into a clean sterilised bottle. Place a stopper or cork in the top and leave to infuse for at least 1 month.

• **Make sure the lemon grass is covered in the oil. If you find things float to the top, try threading the solid ingredients on a cocktail stick and pushing that into the oil.**

SUN-DRIED TOMATO PESTO

I make this Pesto to give to busy friends.

MAKES ABOUT ONE 450 g (1 lb) JAR

1 lemon

2 garlic cloves

225 g (8 oz) sun-dried tomatoes in oil

175 g (6 oz) blanched almonds

1 handful of flat-leaved fresh parsley

1 handful of fresh basil

225 ml (8 fl oz) extra virgin olive oil

175 g (6 oz) freshly grated Parmesan cheese

salt and pepper

1 Using a potato peeler, remove zest from the lemon and put in a food processor. Skin the garlic and add to the lemon zest with the tomatoes, almonds, parsley and basil. If the mixture is too dry add a little of the oil.

2 Slowly pour in the remaining oil. Pour the sauce in a mixing bowl and add the Parmesan cheese, salt and pepper.

3 Pour into a sterilised jar and use diluted with a little cream for pasta.

• Sun-dried tomatoes have a pungent, concentrated tomato flavour. The ones preserved in oil are softened and easy to process. If using the dried ones, allow to soften in a little hot water for 30 minutes, drain and then liquidise.

TARRAGON AND PECAN PESTO

MAKES ABOUT ONE 350 g (12 oz) JAR

1 garlic clove

125 g (4 oz) freshly grated Parmesan cheese

125 g (4 oz) pecan nuts

25 g (1 oz) goats' cheese

1 teaspoon lemon juice

grated rind of 1 lemon

handful of fresh tarragon

6 tablespoons extra virgin olive oil

pepper

1 Put all the ingredients in a food processor and blend together for 2-3 minutes, until smooth.

2 Pour into a sterilised jar and store in the fridge. Serve with freshly steamed spring vegetables, baked cherry tomatoes and pasta.

• Ensure that there is always a layer of oil on top of the pesto in the jar to stop the pesto from drying out.

ROCKET PESTO

MAKES ABOUT ONE 450 g (1 lb) JAR

1 lemon

1 garlic clove

2 large handfuls of rocket

75 g (3 oz) walnuts

75 g (3 oz) blanched almonds

150 g (6 oz) freshly grated pecorino cheese

1 teaspoon balsamic vinegar

salt and pepper

200 ml (7 fl oz) extra virgin olive oil

1 Using a potato peeler, remove zest from the lemon and put in a food processor. Peel the garlic and add to the lemon zest with the rocket, walnuts, almonds, pecorino cheese, vinegar, salt, pepper and oil. Run the machine until the mixture is smooth.

2 Pour into a sterilised jar and use in dressings, sauces and pasta.

• Balsamic vinegar is a particularly fine vinegar with a sweet-sour flavour. It is expensive – compared to a malt vinegar – but a litle goes a long way. The teaspoonful in this recipe is well worth having!

Clockwise from top:
Lemon grass oil on salad; Sun dried tomato pesto on pasta; Tarragon and pecan pesto; Rocket pesto; Fruity olive pate on bread.

Index

Almonds: apple, almond and soured cream cake, 98
artichoke, lemon and almond soup, 37
figs in orange juice with toasted almonds and natural yogurt, 12
home-made toasted almond butter, 122
fragrant almond cake, 107
mange-tout, cannellini and almond salad, 20
rocket and almond pesto on rye toasts, 29
Amaretti, 122
Apples: apple, almond and soured cream cake, 98
hot apple juice with cinnamon, lemon and cloves, 17
Apricot, fig and raisin balls rolled in sesame seeds, 14
Artichokes: artichoke pie with gruyere, 88
artichoke, lemon and almond soup, 37
hot broad beans and artichokes with chilli and herbs, 53
Asparagus with red pepper sauce, 66
Aubergines: aubergine rolls with goats' cheese and tomato, 58
baked aubergine, olive and mozzarella sandwich with basil, 22
baked aubergines with herby spinach and tomato middles, 57

cake of aubergine and courgettes, 92
pickled aubergines, 134
sun dried tomato pesto and pickled aubergine sandwich, 21
Avocado: pickled red onion and avocado sandwich, 30

Bananas: banana and honey super shake, 17
banana curd, 128
hot spiced bananas with amaretto cream, 106
Bean sprout salad with nuts, apples and raisins, 25
Beans: pasta and bean soup, 58
Beetroot: baked beets with a nut and cheese crumb, 52
beetroot and feta sandwich with parsley, 21
Bitter leaves with romesco dressing, 30
Bread: bread gnocchi with rosemary and chervil, 44
ciabatta, 127
flattened bread filled with spinach and olives, 119
focaccia, 115
grissini, 118
hot cinnamon toast, 12
potato pizza bread, 118
prune and chocolate bread, 120
rosemary and basil

buttered toast with grilled cherry tomatoes, 13
rum plum bread, 124
rustic walnut bread, 114
sour dough bread, 114
sweet milk bread with cumin and orange, 123
Broad beans: broad beans and mint with gorgonzola dressing, 22
hot broad beans and artichokes with chilli and herbs, 53
Broccoli: baked shallots with creamy broccoli, 38
broccoli and cauliflower with parmesan butter, 54

Cabbage, mushroom and egg filling, 33
Carrots: carrot, cheese and parsley sandwich with mayo, 21
cheesey carrot and nut bites with sesame seeds, 24
Cauliflower: broccoli and cauliflower with parmesan butter, 54
Celeriac and pecorino filling, 33
Cheese: beetroot and feta sandwich with parsley, 21
brandy, date and orange cream cheese, 124
carrot, cheese and parsley sandwich with mayo, 21
celeriac and pecorino filling, 33

char-grilled vegetables layered with cheeses, 84
cheesey carrot and nut bites with sesame seeds, 24
dolcelatte and lemon dressing, 68
fried four-cheese ravioli, 72
fried mozzarella sandwiches, 26
parsley and mozzarella colzone, 64
poppy seed, celery, gorgonzola and chive filling, 32
ricotta and nutmeg dumplings with gorgonzola sauce, 48
roasted garlic and dolcelatte toasts, 29
roasted red pepper, cream cheese and rocket salad, 26
roasted tomatoes on toast with goats' cheese and coriander, 24
Chestnuts: chestnut soup with chick peas, 61
chocolate and chestnut torte, 103
Chick peas: chestnut soup with chick peas, 61
chick pea stew with Mediterranean vegetables and fennel seeds, 66
Chicory rolls, 40
Chocolate: baked chocolate cheesecake with vanilla and pecan nuts, 102
chocolate and chestnut torte, 103
chocolate polenta cake, 102
prune and chocolate bread, 120
warming hot chocolate, 16
Chutney: coriander, mint and chilli chutney, 131
Coffee: espresso with amaretto and cream, 17
wicked coffee fudge pudding, 98
Courgettes: cake of aubergine and courgettes, 92
layered courgette and barley tortino, 72
warm creamy courgette, coriander and spinach toasts, 25

Dates: brandy, date and orange cream cheese, 124
date and cognac ice cream, 106

Eggs: cabbage, mushroom and egg filling, 33

Fennel under a garlic cheese crumb, 36
Figs: apricot, fig and raisin balls rolled in sesame seeds, 14
dried pears, peaches and figs in red wine, 107
figs in orange juice with toasted almonds and natural yogurt, 12
Florentines, 128
Fromage frais: zesty soufflé's with apricot sauce, 110

Garlic: pasta with garlic, walnut and rocket sauce, 49
rigatoni with garlic, rosemary and mushrooms, 54
roasted garlic and dolcelatte toasts, 29
Glogg, 80
Grapes: black grape cake with olive oil, 104

Hollandaise sauce, 85

Ice cream: date and cognac ice cream, 106
honey ice cream, 99

Leeks: leek and tomato soup with crusty bread and basil, 57
leek, thyme and pistachio soufflés, 85
Lemon grass oil, 134
Lentils: Italian green lentil soup, 60

Mange-tout, cannellini and almond salad, 20

Millet: warm marinated
    millet salad, 20
Miso: vitality spread, 12
Muffins: zesty fruit and nut
    muffins, 14
Mumma, 80
Mushrooms: cabbage,
    mushroom and egg
    filling, 33
  giant stuffed mushrooms
    with pine nuts and sage,
    44
  mushroom burger with
    leeks and blue cheese, 60
  mushroom lasagne with
    roasted peppers and
    ricotta, 96
  mushrooms crostini with
    leeks and artichokes,
    28
  potato and mushroom
    layer cake, 89
  shallot, spinach and
    mushroom tian, 94

Olives: baked aubergine,
    olive and mozzarella
    sandwich with basil,
    22
  deep fried caper-stuffed
    olives, 80
  flattened bread filled
    with spinach and olives,
    119
  fruity olive pate, 134
Onions: baked onions with
    a parsley and parmesan
    stuffing, 76
  pickled red onion and
    avocado sandwich, 30
  pickled red onions, 132

Pancakes: buckwheat
    pancakes, 13
Parsnip, leek and coriander
    soup, 69
Pasta: cake of pasta and
    spinach, 94
  fresh egg pasta, 130
  fresh pasta with spinach,
    nutmeg and pine nut
    filling, 82
  fried four-cheese ravioli,
    72
  grandmother Furiani's
    radicchio lasagne, 95
  mushroom lasagne with
    roasted peppers and
    ricotta, 96
  pasta and bean soup, 58
  pasta with garlic, walnut
    and rocket sauce, 49
  penne with pepper and
    pistachio sauce, 56
  penne with pumpkin and
    pecorino, 46
  rigatoni with garlic,
    rosemary and
    mushrooms, 54
  tagliatelle in a fresh basil
    and walnut sauce, 65
  tagliatelle with saffron
    and mascarpone sauce,
    56
Peaches: baked peaches
    with amaretti, 110
  dried pears, peaches and
    figs in red wine, 107
  peachy yogurt shake, 16
Pears: dried pears, peaches
    and figs in red wine, 107
Pecan nuts: baked
    chocolate cheesecake
    with vanilla and pecan
    nuts, 102

pecan meringue pie with
    caramelised apples, 111
  tarragon and pecan pesto,
    135
Peppers: baked baby
    peppers, 46
  cold peppers stuffed with
    celery, 69
  roasted peppers with a
    pine nut and sultana
    stuffing, 64
  roasted red pepper and
    spinach filling, 33
  roasted red pepper tart,
    76
  roasted red pepper, cream
    cheese and rocket salad,
    26
Pizza: celebration pizzas,
    88
  radicchio and pecorino
    pizza, 77
  white pizza with two
    cheeses and basil, 73
Plums: dried plum gnocchi
    with cloves, 104
  rum plum bread, 124
Polenta: chocolate polenta
    cake, 102
  polenta pie, 86
Poppy seed, celery,
    gorgonzola and chive
    filling, 32
Porridge: fruity porridge,
    16
Potatoes: baked potatoes,
    32
  potato and mushroom
    layer cake, 89
  potato croquettes, 48
  potato pizza bread, 118
Prunes: boozy stuffed
    prunes drizzled with

chocolate, 99
prune and chocolate
bread, 120
Pumpkin: pickled
pumpkin, 132
pumpkin fritters with sage
and parmesan, 52

Radicchio: grandmother
Furiani's radicchio
lasagne, 95
radicchio and pecorino
pizza, 77
radicchio risotto, 53
Raisins: apricot, fig and
raisin balls rolled in
sesame seeds, 14
bean sprout salad with
nuts, apples and raisins,
25
risotto with raisins and
pine nuts, 49
Rice: deep fried risotto
with shallots, orange rind
and mozzarella, 40
radicchio risotto, 53
risotto with asparagus,
basil and peas, 45
risotto with raisins and
pine nuts, 49
Rice noodle cloud with
stir-fried vegetables,
38
Rocket: pasta with garlic,
walnut and rocket sauce,
49
roasted red pepper,
cream cheese and rocket
salad, 26
rocket and almond pesto
on rye toasts, 29

rocket pesto, 135

Salt, fragrant, 131
Scones: walnut scones,
126
Shallots: baked shallots
with creamy broccoli, 38
shallot, spinach and
mushroom tian, 94
Soya milk: banana and
honey super shake, 17
Spinach: cake of pasta and
spinach, 94
flattened bread filled with
spinach and olives, 119
shallot, spinach and
mushroom tian, 94
spinach and cheese
crespolini, 68
Sprouted beans with
Chinese leaf, ginger and
coconut, 61
Sweetcorn: creamy corn
tart with chilli and
coriander, 81

Tahini: vitality spread, 12
Taralli, 126
Tarragon and pecan pesto,
135
Tomatoes: leek and tomato
soup with crusty bread
and basil, 57
roasted cherry tomatoes
with red onions, spinach
and cheese sauce, 41
roasted tomatoes on toast
with goats' cheese and
coriander, 24

rosemary and basil
buttered toast with
grilled cherry tomatoes,
13
sun dried tomato pesto
and pickled aubergine
sandwich, 21
sun dried tomato pesto,
135
sun dried tomato purée,
130
tangy tomato soup with
lemon grass, 37
tomato and mint salad,
28
tomato, hazelnut and
thyme filling, 32

Vegetable stock, 36
Vegetables: char-grilled
vegetables layered with
cheeses, 84

Walnuts: pasta with garlic,
walnut and rocket sauce,
49
rustic walnut bread,
114
tagliatelle in a fresh basil
and walnut sauce, 65
walnut scones, 126

Yogurt: figs in orange
juice with toasted
almonds and natural
yogurt, 12
peachy yogurt shake, 16